D0928129

# A HISTORY OF ISLAM IN 21 WOMEN

# A HISTORY

# OF ISLAM

# IN 21

# WOMEN

## HOSSEIN KAMALY

ONEWORLD

A Oneworld Book

First published by Oneworld Publications, 2019

Copyright © Hossein Kamaly 2019

ISBN 978-1-78607-643-4
eISBN 978-1-78607-632-8

Illustrations © Peter Locke 2019

Typeset by Hewer Text UK Ltd, Edinburgh
Printed and bound in Great Britain by Clays Ltd, Elcograf S.p.A.

Oneworld Publications
10 Bloomsbury Street
London WC1B 3SR
England

MIX
Paper from
responsible sources
FSC® C018072

To five women who define my history: Maryam, Behjat, Afsar, Mitra, and Mojdeh

# CONTENTS

# INTRODUCTION

The idea of writing *A History of Islam in 21 Women* occurred to me on a Christmas morning in London. In the middle of a conversation about women as agents of historical change in the world, my friend showed me a copy of *A History of Britain in 21 Women*. I suggested that the time had come for a history of Islam that similarly focuses on women. Within days, I started planning the book and before long I was offered a contract to write it.

This book is an invitation to think about the history of Islam in general, and women's active and decisive presence in this history. Beginning in seventh-century Arabia, where Islam first took root, the narrative continues to the here and now, as hundreds of millions of humans across the globe claim Islam as their own.

To the skeptic who presumes that Islam, like several other of the world's religions, has allotted to women the "silent" roles of motherhood and homemaking, organizing a history of Islam around them may seem an inconceivable or futile undertaking. Do domestic tasks merit the attention of the historian? They should. Reducing women's history to silence signals poor analysis anywhere and at any time in history. Women's history is human history.

I invite you on an exciting intellectual journey that aims to set the historical record straight. Our point of departure is that in the past and today women have shaped many aspects of the history of Islam and deserve a more central place in the historical narrative. With all these examples from the past, fostering even more visible and more effective roles for women in the present and future of Islam is a quintessential issue of our time.

The following pages present interlinked episodes in the history of Islam through biographical sketches of twenty-one women. Oneworld Publications set the rules of the game by specifying the number, in keeping with the titles in a series heralded by Jenni Murray's highly popular *A History of Britain in 21 Women* (2016) and *A History of the World in 21 Women* (2018). The number twenty-one hints at the contemporary relevance of the material in our time, the twenty-first century.

Doing history by numbers, which means organizing historical narrative around a specific number of people, periods, or objects, can be entertaining as well as enriching. A popular practice today, journalists often convey information through "listicles," articles structured as numbered lists: 7 Signs of Worldwide Climate Change; 9 Dividend Stocks to Buy; 10 Ways to Lose 20 Pounds in 30 Days, etc. Like painting by numbers, however, doing history by numbers has both benefits and limitations.

Here, I use the twenty-one biographies as guideposts. The terrain covered is vast: from the Arabian Peninsula and India to Spain, North Africa, and Nigeria; from Egypt and Syria to Turkey, Indonesia, and Russia; from Iran and Iraq to the United Kingdom and the United States, and others. The women highlighted, who include religious exemplars and political authorities, are too diverse to represent a single ideal or ideal type, and they seldom appear together in general histories of Islam.

# INTRODUCTION

Because I want this book to serve as a broad-based invitation to learn more about the role of women in the history of Islam, I have steered away from the controversy that surrounds some of them and tried to be faithful to primary sources while also drawing on contemporary scholarship. The chronological sequence of biographies in this book moves from five religious exemplars to eight rulers to four women involved in faith movements in the colonial era, and lastly to four whose involvement with Islam remains arguably tangential to their careers in the modern world. This succession roughly reflects the evolution of the history of Islam in available sources. The information that has survived from the seventh to eleventh centuries relates to models of piety and spiritual inspiration, and it is not always clear how much of that material is factual in the historical sense. From the eleventh to seventeenth centuries we have sustained evidence of the lives of identifiable historical women. Multiple chronicles describe the actions of several Muslim queens, regents, and other women who wielded political and military power in their time. Many "Western" or Orientalist histories of Islam stop in the seventeenth century, but since the nineteenth century challenging encounters between Muslim societies and Europe, or the elusive "West", have stirred frequent calls to reform Islam. Nationalism often sought to redefine and renegotiate gender relations on new terms and women participated in reform movements even as they undertook an increasing array of secular occupations. This major shift in activity has influenced the way women are represented in contemporary sources.

I shall return to a discussion of my sources in the Afterword and "Further Reading" suggests some more in-depth studies of the lives and times of our twenty-one women. All translations in the book are my own, except where attributed to others. Throughout, I have kept endnotes to a minimum.

3

# 1

# Khadija
## (ca. 560–619)

## THE FIRST BELIEVER

K hadija was the first believer, the very first *mumin*. She made her mark on the history of Islam very early in the seventh century CE. She believed the message of her husband, Prophet Muhammad, even before he openly started to call the people in the Arabian town of Mecca to the one and only God. With unwavering faith in his vocation, she stood by him in the hardest times, to her dying breath. She witnessed the Prophet's sincerity of heart and nobility of spirit, offered him genuine human love, and bolstered his resolve. Today more than ever, it is important to highlight that the first person to receive the Prophet's message was a woman.

Prophet Muhammad often turned to Khadija for advice. She knew him well and he trusted her. Up to the moment when he accepted his vocation of delivering God's message to his people, marriage to Khadija had been his greatest good fortune. And when that decision shook him to the core, he relied on Khadija's calming compassion and wisdom.

The bustling town of Mecca, a center for regional and long-distance trade, distressed the young Muhammad with its pervasive injustice, moral decay, and spiritual emptiness. He labeled all

5

that he disliked about it as the darkness of ignorance and folly, *al-jahiliya*. By contrast, Khadija was his lodestar, providing love, light, and support. With her backing, he committed himself to good deeds and for a month at a time immersed himself in contemplation and devotional practices, fasting, praying, and helping the poor in and around his hometown.

Sometimes Muhammad withdrew to a cave in a nearby hill. On his return he would first visit the holy site at the heart of Mecca: the Kaaba, and walk round it seven times or more, chanting the mantra, "Here I come my God, here I am. All praise and power is yours."

The Kaaba, also called Bayt-Allah, or the House of Allah, stood as a tribute to God in Mecca and was less than an hour's walk from Khadija's home and workplace. Locals believed that the biblical patriarch Abraham and his first son, Ishmael, had erected it in honor of the God of heaven and earth and the God of Abraham, Ishmael, and Isaac. However, by the seventh century, that cube-shaped monument built for the one and only God functioned like the Pantheon in ancient Rome – as a temple for multiple gods. Inside at least one large statue carved out of reddish-brown stone, maybe carnelian, sat behind a curtain. Outside stood scores of other statues, idols, and effigies. A consecrated well named Zamzam was sunk some forty paces to the east of the Kaaba.

During the seventh century, toward the end of the period that historians call Late Antiquity, a variety of religious beliefs and practices coexisted in the Arabian Peninsula. In the northwestern parts of Arabia, the region known as Hijaz, Christianity and Judaism had followers. However, sources compiled retrospectively by later Muslim writers identify the majority of the population as pagans or polytheists who worshipped multiple deities, often in the form of wooden or stone idols. Many Arab tribes kept a representation of their favored deity inside or outside the Kaaba. At regular times of festival, they gathered at the site, performed various rituals, and asked for protection and good luck. Beyond the Kaaba, natives considered many other sites as holy, including wells, springs, and streams in desert valleys. People came to Mecca from distant parts of the Arabian Peninsula, as far south as Yemen and as far east as the rims of the vast desert aptly known as the Empty Quarter.

Although Mecca was far from the current centers of political power and commercial wealth in Constantinople and Ctesiphon, it was still important, especially at the turn of the seventh century CE, when Arabia was about to witness the birth of what became known as Islam.

One summer night in 610 CE, when Khadija's husband was about forty years old, he cut short his habitual period of seclusion in a cave near Mecca. Something inexplicable had happened. The archangel Gabriel had visited him with a message from the one and only God. Still in shock, he stumbled home. Comforted by Khadija's presence, he confided in her what he had experienced:

> Gabriel appeared to me in a dream-vision. He was carrying a scroll sealed in a brocade with some writing on it. He told me, "Read!" I asked, "What shall I read?" He pressed me in a crushing embrace, like death. Then he let go and commanded, "Read!" I implored, "What shall I read?"[1]

The wording of the original account in Arabic sounds puzzling and the English translation is hardly clearer. After a third such exchange, the angel instructed:

> Read! In the name of your Lord who created,
> Who created humans from a clot.
> Read! And your Lord is most Munificent,
> Who taught by the pen,
> Taught humans what they knew not.[2]

Muhammad told Khadija, "Finally, I recited the writing, and the Angel Gabriel left. Coming through, I felt those words were inscribed on my heart."[3]

Muslim tradition records this momentous epiphany, this encounter with the ineffable and transcendent reality, as the start of Prophet Muhammad's mission as God's messenger – the *mab'ath*. The Angel Gabriel's instructions became part of the Quran, the Muslim Holy Scripture. Accounts of how exactly the Quran was compiled vary, but within a generation after the Prophet Muhammad, the majority of his followers recognized it as a closed and complete record of God's spoken word. These early elements from revelations in the Quran encapsulate some of the fundamental elements of what later became known as Islam: an emphasis on God, the creator; the mystery of creation; the utter dependence of humans on their creator; the creator's absolute generosity; as well as the weight given in the Islamic tradition to knowledge, reading, and writing.

Unsure of what his vision meant, Muhammad worried. He sought Khadija's counsel. Could it have been sheer fantasy? In Mecca, it was the poets who had a reputation for telling tall tales based on their dreams and delusions, and most people thought they were possessed by demons who spoke through them. Crowds gathered to hear them but they were not respected. At home, Muhammad sat by Khadija's side, leaning on her literally and figuratively. Lovingly, she wrapped him in a blanket and comforted him. Listening intently to his account of what had happened, she assured him that he was nothing like those poets. Surely God would never delude a man who helped debtors get out of debt, who fed the hungry, spoke only the truth, and always stood for justice. No, he was no poet. She believed him. She believed in him.

Khadija had married Muhammad more than a decade earlier. Everything about him had impressed her, so much in fact that contrary to custom she took the initiative and asked for his hand in marriage. What had she seen in him? As far as his looks went, the Islamic tradition remembers Prophet Muhammad as a well-proportioned man, neither stout nor skinny, neither short nor too tall. He had a broad forehead, with curved eyebrows, wide-set black eyes, and noticeably long eyelashes. He let his beard grow thick and his hair long. When he smiled, and he smiled often, his lips parted, and his white teeth showed. His face was always radiant. He walked with a spring in his step, leaning forward slightly as if he were walking downhill. People enjoyed speaking with him and found him charismatic. Khadija saw all this in him, and more.

According to the oldest written biography of the Prophet, from around the middle of the eighth century CE, when Khadija heard what had happened to her husband she immediately set out to investigate. She rose to her feet, gathered her garments about her – an expression that in Arabic signals determination – and went to seek advice from her cousin Waraqa, whose wisdom and great learning she admired. In Mecca Waraqa belonged to a small circle known as the *hanifs*, the purists. Regarding themselves as pure-hearted seekers of the truth, the *hanifs* rejected the religious beliefs and practices common in Mecca and instead embraced Abrahamic practices such as walking around the House of Allah and refusing to worship idols. Although no complete copy of the Hebrew Bible – the Mosaic scriptures – was available in Arabic, the *hanifs* knew at least parts of it. At the same time they revered Jesus, though they did not have access to the Gospels in Arabic and did not belong to a Christian church. One of the eclectic elements in the teachings of the *hanifs* was that they expected the advent of a prophet among the Arabs.

When Khadija related what her husband had told her, Waraqa exclaimed, "Holy! Holy! He must be the awaited prophet." Perhaps recalling that the Lord's chosen messenger would receive sealed scrolls and not be able to read them out, Waraqa identified Muhammad as the prophet announced in the Torah and the

Gospels. In some lines of poetry that have come down to us, he expressed joy for the coming of this awaited prophet:

> I persevered and persisted in a
> Remembrance that often evoked tears.
> Now confirming evidence comes from Khadija.
> Long have I had to wait, O Khadija,
> In the vale of Mecca in spite of my hope
> That I might see the outcome of your words.[4]

Recognizing the signs of a prophet, Waraqa told Khadija to encourage and support her husband. He also warned her of inevitable opposition from the enemies of God, who would persecute Muhammad, accusing him of being an imposter, a poet, or a madman and driving him out of his homeland. Nevertheless, salvation was his and for those who followed him in the path of the one true God, the God of Abraham and Jesus. Waraqa's words buoyed Khadija's spirit but his warning worried her. Knowing Meccan society well, she resolved to protect her husband and keep him safe.

Like most of the Arabian Peninsula in the seventh century, Meccan society was tribal. Social capital and standing derived primarily from tribal affiliation, and a person's honor, property, and their life depended greatly on the tribe to which they belonged. A man abandoned by his tribe had much to fear, as did an orphan like Muhammad, even if he belonged to a powerful tribe. And so Khadija was Muhammad's shield. As a wealthy woman with a distinguished tribal pedigree, Khadija in her forties was a force to be reckoned with in Mecca. She used her standing to back her husband at a time when he was most vulnerable. What does that say about Khadija?

Prophet Muhammad and Khadija both belonged to the tribe of Quraysh, whose chiefs controlled Mecca and surrounding areas. Some of the Quraysh were landowners and agriculturalists.

The tribe was large and had many branches, two of which dominated the others. One of these was the Hashemites, the descendants of Hashem who held the honorable title of keepers of the keys of the Kaaba. The other powerful branch was the Umayyads, the descendants of Hashem's nephew Umayya, who dominated the field of commerce. As rival cousins, the Hashemites and the Umayyads vied for resources and honors and were not always friendly with each other.

The Quraysh were not alone in Mecca, however. There were other, less important tribes in the region and Mecca became a hub for men and women from as far north as Syria and as far south as the Yemen, coming in pilgrimage to the spiritually potent Kaaba and the many holy sites in the surrounding desert valleys. Making a promise, taking an oath, or having a vision near the Kaaba and the Zam-Zam well carried much weight and meaning. Year after year, tribesmen came to renew peace treaties, endorse bonds, and, of course, bolster the honor of their tribes. When in Mecca they often used the occasion to conduct business with the locals and with other pilgrims. But whether they were locals or pilgrims, everyone would have recognized someone like Khadija as a prominent Meccan, one owed respect and even deference.

The status of women more generally, however, was fraught and full of contradictions. The tribesmen stigmatized womanhood and considered all things feminine to be weak, fragile, and generally inferior; a father who had daughters but no sons was called childless. Some fathers even buried their infant daughters and then prided themselves on having gotten rid of the shame of having fathered a girl. On the other hand, more women than men in Mecca could read and write and, importantly, could own wealth and property as Khadija certainly did. As both her mother and father belonged to influential branches of the Quraysh, Kadija had capital, connections, children, and honor. She was strong, wise, and independent, and men and women answered to her.

Like other elite members of the Quraysh, Khadija invested in long-distance trade between Mecca and the lands of the Roman Empire in the north. A few years before that fateful night in the summer of 610, Khadija had commissioned Muhammad to supervise a load of goods she was sending to Bostra, the capital of the Roman province of Arabia Petraea. Meccan caravans took leather, animal skins, woolen clothing, clarified butter, and perfumes as far north as present-day Syria and Palestine. Like other Meccan merchants, Khadija sold goods to the Roman army, which needed vast quantities of leather and animal skins.

By all accounts, Khadija had heard about Muhammad's honesty and appreciated it. Her trust proved well placed when he returned from the two-month trade journey with noticeably larger-than-usual profits. The young man had grown up an orphan, having lost his father before birth, his mother at around the age of five, and then his paternal grandfather and guardian when still a child. Despite all the personal hardships he had faced, Muhammad had a strong personality and a generous spirit. Impressed with his character no less than his charm, Khadija offered him her hand or asked for his. He accepted.

At the time of their marriage, he was no more than twenty-five and she no less than twenty-eight years old. She had been married twice before; one marriage had ended in widowhood, the other in divorce. Some say she was widowed twice. She had children from both.

Several later sources claim that Khadija was forty at the time of the marriage, but this ought not be taken literally. In Near Eastern literary traditions extending far back into ancient times, the age of forty is associated with perfection, completion, and culmination. True, at the time of marrying Muhammad, Khadija was a woman of balanced emotional and intellectual capability. But she would go on to deliver five or six children, which, at the time, would have been unlikely for a woman in her fifties or even forties.

In 1989, archeological excavations in Mecca unearthed the remains of a building that is believed to have once housed Khadija's business quarters and the home she kept with Prophet Muhammad, including the room where she gave birth to her children. For over twenty years Khadija and Prophet Muhammad lived in that house along with their children. Other members of the household included a freedwoman, Barakah or Umm Ayman, a freedman Zaid, and the Prophet's cousin Ali.

Of course, Khadija's relationship with Muhammad went beyond partnership, in trade or family. Her reaction to his vocation as a divine messenger reveals the depth of her attachment to him and her confidence in his truthfulness. In a deep sense, her reputation as a discerning businesswoman worked to his advantage.

No doubt, being a prophet was a heavy burden to bear. After that initial revelation in the cave, Muhammad stayed home for days, covered in a thick cloak. And for a while, the revelations stopped coming. Had it been a one-off event? He felt perplexed. But Khadija never doubted that God had chosen him to be his prophet. Eventually, Gabriel returned with a reassuring divine message for the Prophet:

> Your Lord has not forsaken you, and He dislikes you not.
> A better hereafter will be for you, better than what came
> before.
> Your Lord will honor you to your satisfaction.[5]

The divine promise of a better future came with a reminder of the hardships of the past:

> Did He not find you an orphan and shelter you?
> Did He not find you cast away and guide you?
> Did He not find you hard-pressed and deliver plenitude?[6]

The divine protection, guidance, and plenitude in Prophet Muhammad's life was manifest, in part, through Khadija's dedication to him. As recorded in the Quran, God commanded His Prophet to:

> Never maltreat an orphan;
> Never fend off a supplicant;
> And be mindful of your God's gifts.[7]

Khadija's generosity went beyond providing funds and offering him comfort. At home, they prayed together daily, before dawn, at noon, in the afternoon, evening, and night. The Prophet showed Khadija how Gabriel had instructed him to wash his face, arms, and feet before every prayer. She set an example for her own daughters to have faith in the Prophet. She backed him up in public as well. After a visit to Mecca, one eyewitness offered the following account:

> A man came out to pray and stood facing the Kaaba; then a woman came out and stood praying with him; then a young man came out and stood praying with him.[8]

The same traveler recalled hearing:

> The man is Muhammad son of Abd-Allah who says God has sent him with a message [of guidance] and the promise that the treasuries of Persian and Roman emperors will open to him. The woman is his wife, Khadija, the young man, his cousin Ali, who have faith in him.

For three years, Prophet Muhammad delivered God's message only to the members of his own household: Khadija, their daughters, and his adolescent cousin Ali, who lived with them. Meanwhile, the revelation continued.

Guided by the revelation, the Prophet eventually shared his message with the heads of the Quraysh, but only a couple of his uncles took him seriously. A handful of men of means joined the ranks of the early believers, most notably a merchant known as Abu Bakr. For the most part, however, his call to the tribe's notables fell on deaf ears. By contrast, the disenfranchised among the poor, the slaves, and those in Mecca who lacked tribal connections welcomed the Prophet's message. First among them was Zayd, a young man whom Khadija had placed at the Prophet's service. There was also a black slave from eastern Africa, named Bilal, and a wandering truth-seeker from the lands to the east, Salman the Persian.

Like the other believers, Khadija professed faith in the true God alone and accepted Muhammad as God's messenger. This constituted the core belief in the way of life the Prophet proposed, which he called Islam. To the believers, the Quran's simple messages urged them to be pious and kind, but they often had an urgent, even apocalyptic ring to them:

When the sun blurs;
When the stars fall;
When the mountains melt;
And when pregnant camels are abandoned . . .[9]
When the infant girl who was buried alive is asked:
For what sin were your slain? . . .[10]

Whither then do you go?
This is a reminder for all worlds;
For all among you who will to go straight.
And your will depends on the will of God—the Lord of all
    worlds.[11]

Warning the people of the coming divine judgment, the Quran urges them to avoid evil and to do good:

Woe unto bitter-tongued backbiters;
Who hoard riches and count them over.
Thinking riches make them immortal?!
No indeed! But they will be cast in the Pit of Hell.[12]

The leaders of the Quraysh dismissed the message, the messenger, and those who followed him. They feared that the wholesale rejection of all gods but one would undermine their authority and hamper their business prospects. But there was more to their aversion. The Quran criticized them, their beliefs, and their way of life. The Prophet did too. In response, they taunted and tormented Prophet Muhammad and the believers. They tortured some to death and made things difficult for others. Repeatedly, they threw filth at the Prophet and the believers. As a woman of substance, Khadija was at first considered off-limits. Before long, however, even her standing wasn't enough to protect the Prophet's household. Eventually, the leaders of the Quraysh agreed to ostracize the man and those close to him.

For three hard years, the Prophet and his immediate circle were confined to a bare valley outside Mecca, where they had no access to basic necessities. Even food had to be brought to them under cover of darkness. Still Khadija, his wife and confidante, stood by him. Until she died in that bare valley in 619 CE. Three days earlier, the Prophet had lost his uncle Abu Talib, Ali's father. These two had been his main protectors. He called that the bleakest of years, the "year of grief."

After those three years, the Prophet left Mecca. As the Gospels have it, "No prophet is accepted in his hometown." And after Khadija's death Prophet Muhammad had to leave his home. Retrospectively, the year 622 CE came to mark the beginning of the Muslim calendar. A new chapter opened in Muhammad's life. New believers welcomed him in the agricultural oasis of Yathrib, some 400 kilometers northeast of Mecca. The oasis was renamed the City of the Prophet, *Madinat al-nabi*, or, simply the City, Medina.

# KHADIJA

Less than a decade after Khadija died, Prophet Muhammad returned in triumph to Mecca. A decade after that, his followers embarked on an enterprise of world conquest. Fond memories of Khadija lived on with the Prophet, who spoke of her often to his companions. The course of Islam might have been different had she lived longer, but there is no doubt about her legacy: Khadija is a heroine of towering stature in Islamic history.

# 2

# Fatima
## (ca. 612–633)

## PROPHET MUHAMMAD'S
## FLESH AND BLOOD

Prophet Muhammad lovingly said about her, "Fatima is my own flesh and blood." All Muslims speak of Fatima, Prophet Muhammad's daughter, with reverence. Her given name at birth, Fatima, remains a popular name for Muslim girls. Also popular are her many nicknames—Zahra, Tahira, Siddiqa, Mubaraka, Raziya, Zakiya, Sayyida, Batul and others—with variant spellings and pronunciations from place to place.

Not only was Fatima the only surviving child of Prophet Muhammad and Khadija, she had married her father's cousin Ali, after the Prophet the most highly esteemed figure in the eyes of Shia Muslims. Also, she had mothered the venerated leaders or Imams of the Shias. Being able to trace one's lineage back to Fatima, and through her to the Prophet himself, remains a great source of honor for Muslims to this day.

Throughout Muslim history, people often add to Fatima's name the honorific title al-Zahra, "the Radiant One," perhaps to emphasize her own merits apart from her connection to her father, mother, husband, and descendants. Fatima was the youngest of Prophet Muhammad's four daughters. The other three,

Zaynab, Ruqayya, and Umm Kulthum predeceased him, and a son he had had died in infancy. As the only surviving child, Fatima was very dear to her father.

The precise date of her birth remains uncertain, like many other specific details about the early decades of Islamic history. Deciding the time, place or other fine points of some important events can be a matter of doctrine rather than historical evidence. For example, historians differ on whether Fatima's birth occurred before or after the beginning of her father's mission as a divine messenger in 610 CE. Most Shia chroniclers, place her birth a few years after the beginning of Prophet Muhammad's mission, rather than up to five years before. Setting her birth after the beginning of her father's prophetic work elevates her status more than if she had been born beforehand. Fatima's biography is interwoven with that of her father. Chroniclers of Prophet Muhammad's life, beginning decades after his lifetime in the eighth century, offer precious little information on Fatima beyond the fact of the Prophet's love for her. Responding to the urgent concerns of their time, these authors focused on political matters, especially the Prophet's conduct as a political and military leader had during warfare, that seemed most relevant in the age of conquest, as Muslim rule expanded. To the detriment of future generations, they neglected much of the real-life detail that had been remembered by eyewitnesses

However, two episodes from Fatima's childhood stand out in the earliest chronicles of the Prophet's life. When her mother, Khadija, died in 619 CE, the little girl was inconsolable. The Prophet calmed her by assuring his young daughter that Angel Gabriel had revealed to him that Khadija had gone to a better place. The Compassionate God had assigned a grand pavilion to Khadija in Paradise, with brilliant pearls hanging from the ceiling. Fatima always believed what the Prophet said. The second incident reflects the trauma she experienced in witnessing the way the Meccans mistreated her beloved father. The young girl gently caressed her father's face as a mother would care for her child.

Fatima and her sisters joined their father in 622 CE, shortly after he migrated from Mecca to Medina. This migration, or *hijra*, signaled a turning point in the history of Islam, and eventually came to mark the beginning of the Islamic calendar. A year later, upon her father's recommendation, Fatima married Ali, the Prophet's cousin. After Khadija, the very first believer, Ali was the second believer in Prophet Muhammad and his message. Ali's father had sent him to stay with the Prophet, and with the help of Khadija, Ali had practically grown up under the Prophet's direct care and remained absolutely loyal to him.

Fatima married Ali in Medina, during the first year of *hijra*. Every aspect of their union has been subjected to doctrinal interpretation and imbued with hidden meaning. However, we have some first-hand recorded historical detail. Given the doubt about the year she was born, Fatima may have been as young as nine or as old as nineteen at the time of her marriage, and at various times, this number has had implications in Islamic law in deciding the ideal age of marriage.

Another lesson from this wedding was that the Prophet wanted marriage to be easy. This showed in the way he handled the union of two people he loved dearly – his daughter Fatima and his cousin Ali. The Prophet instructed Ali to sell his military armor and to buy household items, including a wool-stuffed Egyptian cotton mattress, cushions, a simple floor covering, a water-flask, and some earthenware. Nothing ostentatious. According to custom, days after the wedding the bride's family hosts a feast, the *walima*. The Prophet kept that simple too, offering his guests a very plain meal.

When Fatima was married, the Prophet made sure she lived close by, in fact right next door. She had two sons, Hasan and Husayn, who were born during the second and third years after *hijra* respectively. She had two daughters as well and the Prophet loved them all. They were his family, members of his household, his *ahl al-bayt.*

From 622 to 632 CE, Fatima stood witness as her father delivered his divine message, guided his followers and gave shape to the community of believers. She attended the mosque, a sacred space where her father talked to his people, consulted with them and led them in prayer. Her young boys played with him, even climbing on his back when he prostrated himself in prayer.

What we know of the early community of Muslims in Medina stresses their hardships, the shortage of provisions and the constant threat of another face-off with the nonbelievers. As happens, married life had its own complications. Ali, strong as he was, earned low wages. During the first couple of years of their marriage, Fatima's palms were blistered and calloused from housework and manual chores, such as grinding corn with pestle and mortar and tending domestic animals.

As a gesture of love and respect, the Prophet kissed his daughter's hands every time she came over to visit him or when he went to visit her. However, as sources emphasize, when Fatima complained about her work and asked whether she could hire a servant, the Prophet taught her a prayer to ease her pain instead. He said:

> O Fatima, I shall offer you a better alternative. After every prayer, remember to express thanks to God (thirty-three times), to say God's praise (thirty-three times), and bear witness that there is no god but the real God (thirty-three times), and repeat that God is great (thirty-four times).[1]

Such reports of what the Prophet said and did in specific cases, for example when asked for something or some advice, played an increasingly important role in the history of Islam. These recollections of the Prophet's exemplary conduct shaped the ethical world view of his followers. Later, from the eighth century CE, they became known as hadith.

The hadith quoted here about the Prophet teaching how to call on God in time of hardship has taken other forms as well, and for centuries it has guided countless Muslim women and men in their practice of remembering God in daily life.

The Prophet taught Ali and Fatima, and all his followers, that in all kinds of hardship they should call to God, and only God, in gratitude, praise and supplication. The Prophet was always available to bring peace and provide hope. The emphasis on these details in historical sources has been taken by many as a sign of the Prophet's willingness to impart lessons to Muslim families. As he put it, "The best among you is the one who treats family the best." In arbitrating between his daughter and his son-in-law, both of whom he loved dearly, the Prophet often took the side of Fatima – a lesson for all men, of all times. He said, "Women prevail over good men, and lowly men prevail over women." Another lesson, perhaps not as explicit, was the Prophet's preference that men should not take more than one wife. Polygamy, the practice of taking multiple wives at the same time, was common practice in Mecca and Medina before Islam, and remained so after. When the Prophet died, he had nine wives. However, on the insistence of the Prophet, Ali did not take another wife as long as he was married to Fatima.

However, these and similar reports about the early history of Islam, including the hadith, perhaps provide more detail than was actually known, in a desire to show how things *should* have happened in the past, and, more often, how things *ought* to take place at all times.

Fatima loved her father with all her soul. Watching him on his sick bed during his final days, she wept and recited lines from a beautiful poem that the Prophet's uncle, her father-in-law, had addressed to him years before:

Silver clouds beg for water from his bright face
He who defends orphans and protects widows.
He is always calm, always wise, always prudent;
Never withholding his kindness, wisdom, and generosity.

Smiling at his daughter, the Prophet said, "Recite the Quran instead."

Fatima was a strong-willed and able-bodied woman: she bore five children, ran a busy household and made two journeys to Mecca. From early on, most sources portray the Prophet's daughter as a selfless, giving woman. Accounts of her life show that despite grinding hardship, she preferred to go hungry herself and feed more needy members of the community with the little she had. The same voices that insist on denying or silencing the presence of women in Islamic history in general have sought to depict her as a feeble and passive victim of circumstance. However, Fatima's powerful character is evident in her conduct immediately after the death of her father in 632 CE, when she found herself in the middle of the crisis that broke out when it came to deciding who should become his successor. In the judgment of a leading scholar of early Islam, "No event in history has divided Islam more profoundly and durably than the succession to Muhammad."[2]

While Ali went out to make the burial arrangements, a dozen or so men gathered at the door of Fatima's home. Most of them had been companions of the Prophet. They clamored that Ali should rise to the occasion and take charge of the Muslim community. He was their choice for the Prophet's successor, or *khalifa* (caliph). Those men formed the core of the Followers of Ali, sometimes translated as the Party or Shia of Ali. Notable companions of the Prophet supported Ali, including the Prophet's uncle Abbas, Ali's disciples Abu-Dhar and Maysam the Date-seller, as well as Zubayr and Salman the Persian.

Of course, no one doubted Ali's closeness and loyalty to the Prophet. His record of service, especially his bravery on the battlefield, spoke for itself. Moreover, being married to the Prophet's daughter weighed in his favor. Some even recalled that, on the journey back to Medina from his last pilgrimage to the Kaaba, the Prophet himself had hinted that he wanted Ali to succeed him. In principle, the Prophet's tribesmen, the Quraysh, accepted hereditary succession as the norm. Since the Prophet had no surviving sons, the Shia of Ali contended that the right now belonged to Fatima and her husband.

However, elsewhere in Medina a larger crowd had assembled to decide the issue. They preferred another close companion of the Prophet as *khalifa*. Abu Bakr, the Prophet's old friend and father-in-law, also had an outstanding record and a stellar reputation. Ali's elder by more than twenty years, Abu Bakr also enjoyed widespread respect. He, too, was among the very first believers, in fact he was the first free adult male believer (after the first believer Khadija, who was a woman, Ali who had been a boy at the time, and Zayd who was a freed slave). Unlike most tribesmen of the Quraysh, Abu Bakr had embraced Muhammad as God's messenger, risking his own social standing. The Prophet called him his true friend. He had stood by the Prophet in Mecca and spent much of his wealth to support his cause.

Abu Bakr made his way towards Fatima's house, knowing how important it was to have her support. The fierce-looking men who accompanied Abu Bakr had decided to make sure that Ali shook hands with him. In Arab custom the ritual handshake, or offering the *bay'a*, signaled a promise of loyalty. Should Ali and his small band of followers refuse, the men with Abu Bakr threatened to burn Fatima's house down. In spite of the intimidating presence of torch-wielding armed men, Ali refrained from violence, aiming to maintain the integrity of the community of Muslims that had just lost its leader and Prophet. However, Fatima protested. Standing in the doorway, she kept crying out her father's name. How did they dare show such disrespect? She reprimanded them:

> You have left the body of the Apostle of God with us and you have decided among yourselves without consulting us, without respecting our rights!

Ali backed up Fatima. As long she was alive, he withheld his *bay'a*. Mindful of Ali's closeness to the Prophet and respecting Fatima's standing in the Muslim community, Abu Bakr accepted the decision and ordered his men to disperse. But pressure continued to mount.

An enormous schism emerged in Muslim history based on this decision over Ali's right of succession, although there was never any actual battle between Ali and Abu Bakr themselves. It took much longer for the Muslim community to divide along the lines that only later became known as the Shia and Sunni denominations.

A few days later, when Fatima went to claim what the Prophet had bequeathed to her specifically, Abu Bakr met her with a flat refusal. She reminded him that the Prophet had given her a piece of fertile land in the agricultural oasis named Fadak. This was an agricultural village three or four days by camel to the northeast of Medina. The Prophet had received the land at Fadak as a gift, probably in 629, and had then given it to his daughter. However, Abu Bakr recalled hearing the Prophet say that after he died whatever he had left ought to be given away as charity. He insisted that prophets did not bequeath any material inheritance.

After the unhappy exchange with her father's old companion, Fatima took her protest to the wider community of the Prophet's followers. Historical sources record a speech that she delivered to publicly object to what she saw as a deviation from the Prophet's true legacy. In her strident speech about Fadak, Fatima recited passages from the Quran that acknowledge the right of a man's children, including daughters, to inherit property: "From what is left by parents and those nearest related, there is a share for men, and a share for women."[3]

Addressing Abu Bakr, she asked, "Is it in the Book of God that you inherit from your father and I do not inherit from my father? . . . Does not the Quran command that you should 'render to the kindred their due rights'?"[4] Turning to community of believers she said, "You who have embraced Islam, why should you fail to defend my right? Why the indifference toward the injustice being done to me?"

Naturally, the Shia of Ali took Fatima's side. Along with emphasizing Ali's right to succeed the Prophet as caliph, the Shia supported Fatima's claim to Fadak. However, they remained a minority.

Fatima's health deteriorated quickly. Hearing of this, Abu Bakr wished to visit her and reconcile. It remains unclear, however, whether she accepted; Shia historians maintain that she never did. Chronicles agree that she refused to meet with any of the Prophet's wives and other women of the tribe of Quraysh. Fatima died in the year 633 CE. Like the year of her birth, the exact day of her death remains in doubt. Some sources say she died seventy-five days after the Prophet, some say ninety-five days. She was between eighteen and twenty-eight years old. Ali buried her himself, not disclosing the exact location of her tomb because she had instructed him to keep it a secret. To this day the Shia religious calendar marks more than one day as a somber remembrance of her loss.

Abrogating tribal custom in Arabia, Prophet Muhammad expressed love and respect for his daughter. While detractors taunted him for not having any sons, the Quran assured him that it was the line of his enemies that would end, not his:

In the Name of God, the Compassionate, the Merciful
Behold! We have given you abundant beneficence.
So, pray to your Lord, and bring an oblation.
Indeed, it is your enemy who remains cut off from posterity.[5]

Commentators on the Quran have glossed on the phrase "abundant beneficence," "plenitude of goodness," or *Kawsar* in Arabic. Some say that it refers to a fountain or a gushing spring in Paradise. Others, including most Shias, identify the divine gift of abundant beneficence with Fatima.

# 3

# Aisha

## (ca. 615–678)

## "GET HALF OF YOUR RELIGION FROM HER"

Aisha, daughter of Abu Bakr, was still a child when her father betrothed her to his friend the Prophet Muhammad. The young Aisha was married to him in late 623 or early 624. Some sources say she was five years old, others nine or older, but, as was often the case in medieval writings, these numbers probably had a symbolic significance, conveying purity and innocence rather than an exact age. In the same way, although Aisha never bore a child, the Quran describes her, along with the other wives of the Prophet, as a mother to the believers.[1] Sources agree that Aisha had a prodigious memory and a sharp intellect. So, after the Prophet died in 632, she had a lot to say about him, his teachings, and especially his conduct in private. He confided in her repeatedly, sought her counsel and praised her qualities to others. Over time, he expressed a special affection for her and is said to have died with his head on her lap.

For centuries biographers, historians and preachers have spoken about Aisha as a daughter, wife and mother. Like so much about the first two centuries of Islam in general, what we know about Aisha comes to us through their comments and reflections, often tainted with sectarian coloring. Given the importance of the period, the notion that we can reconstruct or reimagine that past as it really was remains both deeply desired and all but unattainable.

Much of what is known about Aisha is the result of her proximity to the Prophet and her close eyewitness reports about the evolution of his mission in Medina. After his death, she spoke about how he shepherded his flock, maintained peace with various factions in Medina, meted out justice, and when necessary went to war with adversaries.

When the Prophet died, Aisha was easily the most influential of his surviving wives. Both during the Prophet's years in Medina and after he was gone, Aisha made her voice heard on a range of issues, by raising questions and taking positions on matters of importance to the community. When it came to women, she was the prime authority, with her first-hand reports on what she had heard the Prophet say.

Some sources record that the Prophet once approvingly advised, "Get half of your religion from this ruddy-cheeked woman."[2] "Ruddy-cheeked woman" was one of his several endearing nicknames for her. Aisha also commentated on the Quran, pointing out the preferred ordering of passages in the scripture as well as the proper reading and writing of certain words and phrases. Before its final compilation, commonly dated to the 650s, she may have had a partial or complete codex of the Quran prepared for herself. By the mid-ninth century CE, when Muslims took stock of hadith or reports about the sayings and conduct of the Prophet, some traced as many as 2,210 to Aisha herself, and 1,200 of these through her back to the Prophet.[3] These numbers indicate her acknowledged position as one of the most prolific sources of eyewitness reports about the Prophet.

Even powerful men among the Prophet's companions could hardly silence or ignore Aisha's voice. She had strong allies among the two principal groups in the community: the Migrants, or *mohajirun*, who had joined the Prophet in Medina around 622; and the Helpers, or *ansar*, who had invited the Prophet to Medina and supported him there. Besides, her personal authority was hard to undermine, especially given that the Prophet had come to her defense when some men in Medina, including a few of his companions, had questioned her chastity and moral probity, in an episode the early chronicles called the Slander Affair (or sometimes the Necklace Incident).

This is what had happened. The Prophet and some of his companions were in the habit of taking their wives with them when they ventured out of Medina. Returning to Medina from a military campaign alongside the Prophet, Aisha found herself left behind the caravan and stranded in the wilderness. On a midway stop, she had gone to wash in the morning, but when she returned, her party had left. Sources compiled later quote her as saying:

> I checked my chest and noticed that the necklace of Yemen beads which my mother had given me was missing. I went back to look for my necklace and missed the caravan when I came back. I never thought the men would leave without me. However, those who had mounted the litter on camelback had failed to realize I was not in it . . . Back then, women were small and did not weigh much. They had little to eat . . . I was a small and light woman too . . . So, I wrapped myself in my sheet and lay down, falling asleep as I hoped for them to come back and get me.

It was usual for caravans to have multiple segments: a vanguard group rushed faster in the front, the main body traveled at a regular pace, then a slower, trailing party lagged behind. After some time, a young man arrived from behind the main caravan. He recognized Aisha, because he had seen her before, when the Prophet had not yet prescribed *hijab*, the requirement that women should appear covered in public. Helping her climb up on his camel, the man delivered her home to the Prophet, all within a matter of hours.

Seeing that a young man had accompanied Aisha to town, one of the men in Medina who held a grudge against the Prophet saw this as an opportunity to attack him where it hurt most. He and his clique started rumors against Aisha, insinuating that something inappropriate had happened between her and the man who brought her back to town. Dishonoring a man's wife was, and continues to be, a grave insult in Muslim society. However, contrary to what Aisha's slanderer wished for, the Prophet did not even flinch, let alone kill or beat his wife according to pre-Islamic Arab custom. He did not even divorce Aisha, although this seemed like the least controversial option. Instead, the Prophet seized on the occasion to deliver God's reprimand to those who accuse women of moral transgression without proof: "Those who slander married women without producing four witnesses, flog them with eighty stripes; and reject their evidence ever after: for they are wicked transgressors."[4] Requiring four eyewitnesses for an alleged private act made it hard to make such a grave accusation; in much the same way, Jesus' response when asked about an accused adulterer, condemned to be stoned to death, was to say: "Let him who is without sin among you cast the first stone at her."

Aisha's slanderers have gone down in Islamic history with a most shameful title, the hypocrites. They claimed and pretended to have faith but in fact acted in bad faith, as two-faced dissimulators or masked unbelievers. Aisha's exoneration and the denunciation of her slanderers elevated her position in the eyes of the community around the Prophet.

So when Prophet Muhammad took his last breath in her chamber in 632, many members of the Muslim community accepted her testimony that the Prophet had wished her father to lead the community as his successor or caliph (*khalifa*). Later sectarian chroniclers disagree about the exact date of the Prophet's death, whether it took place in late May or early June, but they all agree on the decisive significance of Aisha's intervention on the matter of the Prophet's succession. Sunni chroniclers highlight how she prevented the spread of confusion. By contrast, Shia chroniclers stress that she stood against the Prophet's daughter Fatima, his son-in-law Ali, and a chosen group of the Prophet's companions. The impact of her intervention in the history of Islam remains uncontested.

Watching developments from the vantage point of an insider, as the Prophet's widow and his successor's daughter, Aisha continued to make herself heard. On many occasions she dismissed what other companions of the Prophet reported about his sayings and actions; especially when those companions, most of them men, talked about the Prophet's personal conduct towards his wives or what he had instructed women to do, Aisha questioned how they could have heard, seen or known anything about it. Women had been present; men had not.[5] For example, she objected when one of the companions insisted that women ought to undo their braids and then touch their hair only with wet hands, as part of the preparation for daily prayers. Scoffing at his proposition, Aisha reportedly said, "While he was at it, how come he did not require that women ought to shave their heads?!" She added, "When I prepared myself for prayers alongside the Prophet, we used water from the same bucket for ablution, and [he approved as I] passed my wet hand over my braids three times without undoing them."[6]

Once, a male companion declared that he would have to stop praying if any of three things stood or crossed in front of him: dogs, donkeys or women. Aisha lambasted him, saying, "He failed to listen properly, and should you ask him a question, he is bound to answer incorrectly."[7] She added, "You compare us now to asses and dogs. In the name of God, I have seen the Prophet saying his prayers while I was there, lying on the bed between him and the *qibla*. And in order not to disturb him, I didn't move."[8] Aisha clearly understood and rejected the implications of treating women as symbolic barriers to connection with God, alongside dogs and donkeys.

After her father died in 634, Aisha maintained her elevated social standing. Abu Bakr's successor, caliph Umar, who held the reins of the community for the next decade, continued to hold Aisha in high esteem.

The reign of caliph Umar, 634–644, opened a new chapter in the history of Islam. Before him, Abu Bakr had rooted out opposition to Islam throughout the Arabian Peninsula. In what became known as the Wars Against Apostasy, or *ridda* wars, he quashed revolts that had erupted as far south as Yemen. Caliph Umar followed in the footsteps of his predecessor, but with even more vigor and much more widely. Launching large-scale conquests beyond the Arabian Peninsula, keeping detailed records of the spoils of war, fixing the year of *hijra* as the origin of the Islamic calendar, and appointing judges over newly conquered territories were some of caliph Umar's major accomplishments. He committed himself to glorifying the Prophet's legacy. While he strongly disapproved of people sharing their memories of the Prophet, especially in writing, he did not apply this to Aisha's contribution.

A couple of centuries later, Muslim tradition preserved some of the reports attributed to Aisha but discarded or disregarded others. Of the roughly 1,200 reports about the Prophet traced to her, only 174 appear in one of the canonical collections of Sunni hadith and a mere 54 in another.[9] The Shia tradition usually downplays Aisha's reports altogether.

Once caliph Umar was killed in 644, by a disgruntled man who had been captured during the conquests, Aisha once again weighed in. She offered her support to Uthman, another respected companion of the Prophet. Under him, the conquests continued. After Uthman, Aisha wished to weigh in again. This time it was different.

One of the reasons why, apart from their sectarian views, chroniclers have suppressed Aisha's voice has to do with her revolt against a ruling caliph, Ali. In June 656, Prophet Muhammad's third successor Uthman was murdered. His greatest contribution during his time as the third caliph, between 644 and 656, was to oversee the compilation of standard codices of the Quran. Through a meticulous process, he had all the passages compiled and authenticated by the early 650s CE. When he was attacked in his home, the 76-year-old Uthman was reciting from one of those codices of the Quran that he had prepared. Medina fell into disarray. Members of the community came to Ali, imploring him to take over command of the Muslims as caliph. A handful of Uthman's kinsmen moreover demanded that Ali should have the murderers arrested and handed over to them for revenge.

In spite of Prophet Muhammad's teaching that the quest for truth and justice ought to take precedence over all kinds of prejudice, including tribal bias, angry men from the Umayyad branch of the tribe of Quraysh insisted on avenging the blood of their kinsman, Uthman. A few key companions of the Prophet agreed. But Ali refused, saying that bloodshed had to stop. War broke out. For the first time, Muslims confronted one another on the battlefield. Such a violation of peace in the community of believers was called a *fitna*.

Aisha was on a pilgrimage to Mecca when she heard the news of Uthman's murder. She positioned herself on the side of two of the Prophet's companions who had been close to her father, namely Talha and Zubayr. She supported the demand that Uthman's blood be avenged. She opposed Ali's decision. Riding on a camel, she set out to take hold of the garrison town of Basra, hundreds of kilometers away to the north in present-day Iraq. Thirteen thousand men rallied around her and she addressed a large crowd at the mosque of Basra. However, the effort failed. Crushing the opposition in what became known as the Battle of the Camel, Ali still showed utmost respect for Aisha and sent her home unharmed. In the end, he proclaimed a general amnesty for all those who threw down their arms. He then spent some days on the battlefield, solemnly burying the dead of both sides. He wept when he saw the bodies of Talha and Zubayr, reminding onlookers that the two had fought many a battle on the Prophet's side.

The trauma resulting from the face-off between the Prophet's close companions in the Battle of the Camel can hardly be exaggerated. Historically, reports that circulated about this event and the value-judgments they expressed or implied divided the followers of Ali, known as Shia Muslims, and others. Some Shias went as far as insulting Aisha, although Sunnis, and mainstream Shias both condemn such disrespect. However, the common ground between many conservatives on both sides of the divide has been that women ought to be kept away from politics.

Reportedly, an old companion of the Prophet Muhammad, who lived in Basra and had witnessed the Battle of the Camel, said he had heard the Prophet say, "Those who entrust power [mulk] to a woman will never know prosperity."[10] According to this companion, called Abu Bakra, the Prophet said this when people told him that the Persian Sasanian dynasty had named a woman as ruler.

The Moroccan sociologist Fatima Mernissi (1940–2015) was skeptical:

> Abu Bakra must have had a fabulous memory, because he recalled [these lines] a quarter of a century after the death of the Prophet, at the time that the caliph 'Ali retook Basra after having defeated Aisha at the Battle of the Camel.[11]

Mernissi casts doubt on the authenticity of what she calls "opportune traditions"[12] but this hadith has had tremendous impact on the writing of history. Its effect on the actual practice of power by women has been less direct (as will become clear in the following pages). Nevertheless, we should bear in mind that most narratives about this formative period of Islam were all carefully reworked to establish some political or theological point. Unsurprisingly, references to Aisha continue to overshadow Muslim views on women, politics and the role of women in politics.

# 4

# Rabia al-Adawiyya
## (ca. 717–801)

## THE EMBARRASSMENT OF RICHES,
## AND ITS DISCONTENTS

In the history of Islam, the eighth century CE marks a watershed, a momentous transition from the Arabian empire of the Umayyad dynasty to the Muslim commonwealth under the early Abbasid caliphs. In the course of this decisive dynastic transition, many aspects of what we know as Islam came to be defined or redefined, including the early formulations of Islamic law. The conquests that caliph Umar had launched more than a century earlier had reached a high point. Geographically, Muslim rule extended far and wide. More people were being born into Islam in Muslim-ruled territories stretching from Iberia to Central Asia.

Within a couple of generations, multiple strands of pietism, asceticism, and mysticism converged and coalesced into a distinct body of beliefs, behavior, and traditions known as Sufism. Rabia al-Adawiyya of Basra was a celebrated female Sufi, or follower of Sufism. She witnessed and experienced this transformation firsthand. For over a millennium, the memory of this woman Sufi has inspired the many articulations of Sufism in the history of Islam.

Our sources mix fact and fiction about Rabia. It is not even clear when exactly she lived, but even the myths that have reached

39

us and surround the kernel of truth still contain valuable scraps of information about her and her time. Rabia's life and legend represent the evolution of an inward-looking and spiritual articulation of Islam. Stories about her tell us how, with a potent combination of ascetic restraint and mystical passion, Sufism integrated many existing and evolving traditions.

When Rabia was born, in or around 717 CE, a generation after Aisha's death in 678, a lot had changed since the early days of Islam. The sense of communal unity and solidarity in faith that Prophet Muhammad's charismatic presence instilled in the believers had waned. His core message of earnest turning towards God and the afterlife had faded. Leaders of the Umayyad branch of the tribe of Quraysh claimed to be the rightful caliphs, building on the support they had received from Aisha during and after the Battle of the Camel. Based in Damascus, the Umayyads spearheaded massive campaigns of conquest in the name of Islam and the Prophet. By the 640s, vast territories extending from Egypt to parts of present-day Iran had already been conquered. Taxes, tributes, and other revenues extracted from conquered lands flooded the coffers of the caliphs. Tens of thousands of subjects were taken into captivity and relocated from their homelands. By Rabia's time, the children of those captured and relocated men and women had grown into adults in towns far from their ancestral homes, many in Iraq and Syria. Most of them hardly knew what Islam meant or what it took to be a Muslim. By then, none of the Companions who had seen the Prophet in person was still living. Those who retained even a faint recollection of the Prophet, linked it to what they had heard from their parents, grandparents, and other elders. Faced with urgent questions and pressing dilemmas, they often wondered, "What is faith?" "Who is a good Muslim?" "What would the Prophet say?"

Not only in Medina and Mecca, where the Prophet had once lived, but also in other towns, men and women contributed answers to these and related questions. Rabia was one of the most remarkable of such individuals; she lived in what is now Iraq, a bastion of Islam at the time.

Founded in the late 630s as a garrison for troops, by the early eighth century Basra had developed into a bustling center of trade and intellectual life in southern Iraq. People of many different languages and ethnic backgrounds called it home. By the 750s a large part of the populace had become Muslim[1] but most of the new converts still continued their previous beliefs and practices as Jews, Christians, Zoroastrians, Manicheans, Sabeans, and others.

Many pious individuals focused their efforts on the preservation of reliable, if incomplete, memories of the Prophet and his exemplary conduct – the *sunna*. They collected reports of what he did and how he acted. Such reports were known as hadith, and the people who centered their lives on the collection and sharing of hadith became known as the hadith-folk. The representation of the Prophet and his teachings through hadith soon came to define Islam. The earliest written biography of Prophet Muhammad, as well as pioneering works on Muslim theology and law, date to this era.

A collection of inauthentic hadith also circulated. Local stories took on new lives, sometimes disguised as hadith. Responding to the sensitivities and sensibilities of the common people, popular preachers and itinerant storytellers readily attributed words to the Prophet that he had not uttered. Perhaps they wished he had. Who could tell an authentic hadith from a spurious story? At the time, no exacting method to separate them was available yet.

Competition over defining Islam and speaking for it was not a mere intellectual exercise. The political stakes were high. The hadith-folk and others clashed with each other doctrinally, politically, and sometimes physically. The 700s saw revolutionary upheavals and rapid transformation against a colorful background of sectarian rivalry, cut-throat competition, and brazen conflict.

Eventually, the Abbasid revolution overthrew the Umayyad caliphate in 750. By then, the world-changing campaigns known as the Islamic conquests had reached unforeseen frontiers. Looking out from the magnificent city of Baghdad, the Abbasid capital from 762, there were Muslim outposts and garrison towns as far east as Gansu and Canton in China, and as far west as the Iberian Peninsula, penetrating well into what we know today as Portugal and Spain. Wealth kept pouring in, especially from long-distance trade. As reflected in the tales told by Scheherazade in *One Thousand and One Nights*, extravagance and worldly excess pervaded the newborn Abbasid caliphate. Still, happiness remained as fragile as ever. The change of dynasty had turned fortunes around, often violently. Many a former prince changed into a pauper. Before their eyes people saw treasures amassed by sheer luck or hard work vanishing as easily as they had come, with the sinking of a ship, a fire in the storehouse, or simply by death. As at similar moments in human history, the embarrassment of riches and related anxieties haunted the age.

Addressing the anxieties and insecurities of her time, Rabia preached in and outside mosques in Basra, often reciting poems about the fragility of life and the urgency of turning to God. Her major contribution was to speak of the divine in loving terms. She was an ascetic and a renunciant, someone who had renounced the society in which they lived, one of the many men and women who called for severe spiritual self-discipline and abstained from all forms of worldly indulgence. What set Rabia apart was that, beyond the fear of God, she stressed and expressed a passionate love for God. A prose version of a short poem attributed to her reads:

You, I love two-fold: What I expect of myself, and what I hope for from you. I expect to keep focused on savoring your memory and to free myself from everything else. I hope you will remove all veils, that I may see you. I deserve no praise for either this or that. Praise for both belongs solely to You.[2]

The love of God, as Rabia understood it, nullifies all fears and all desires. She asks:

O Lord, should I worship you for fear of punishment, then burn me in hellfire. Should I worship you for reward, then keep me out of Paradise. But I worship you only for you. So, do not withhold from me your Eternal Beauty.

To symbolize her view that love and fear of God should not be inspired by desire for Paradise or terror of hell, Rabia is depicted in stories carrying a torch and a bucket of water, resolved to set fire to the gardens of Paradise and extinguish the flames of hell to remind people that they should love God only for God.

Rabia emphasized the need to know one's true self and to embrace the spiritual realm within. She called people to piety, humility, and poverty, insisting that they should not concern themselves with physical appearances and should renounce all worldly attachments. The worldly excesses of the caliphate in Baghdad ran counter to the Sufi emphasis on inwardness and humility. This meant that, from the beginning, Sufism had an explicit political significance.

Rabia advocated exclusive devotion to God coupled with utter reliance on Him. Integrating asceticism and mysticism, she spoke of God not only as the ultimate source of power but also as the eternal and everlasting fount of love: the consummate beloved. This distinct combination of asceticism and mysticism characterizes Rabia and other early Sufis.

Already in the eighth century, some renunciants in Basra, Kufa and elsewhere had taken to wearing a thin cloak of rough wool, known as a *suf* in Arabic. It was cheap, unostentatious, and quite uncomfortable on the skin. The word *Sufi* may refer to this choice of outfit and to the renunciant and self-denying practices that went with it. They fasted as many days of the year as they could, and held long night vigils alone. The Sufis saw life as a journey that had to begin with turning away from worldly attachments and directing everything into the path of God. The ultimate destination was reaching God's presence, and that took a dissolution of one's self.

Rabia stands tall in the history of Sufism, which is sometimes characterized as a manifestation of the mystical dimension of Islam. Over the past hundreds of years, Sufism has changed, undergoing multiple phases, reflecting the peculiarities of different times and places. But almost everywhere and always, Sufis have held Rabia in high esteem. The most detailed portrait of her appears in a thirteenth-century Sufi work of hagiography by Attar of Nishapur (d. ca. 1217), translated as *Memorial of God's Friends*. In nineteenth-century Nigeria, the female educator Nana Asmau (1793–1865) venerated Rabia, along with other female spiritual leaders from the time of the Prophet to her own contemporaries. And throughout the world, Rabia's verses are sung on the street and on screen, as when the twentieth-century Egyptian diva Umm Kulthum sang verses attributed to the eighth-century mystic in a classic of Arab cinema.

There is abundant – though sometimes contradictory – material on Rabia's life and legend. Some sources claim that during Rabia's childhood, when a famine struck Basra, her father sold her into slavery. Some add that she served briefly as a slave owner's singing girl. Others describe her as a woman with servants herself. Several female orators and renunciants named Rabia are widely known, and more than one shares the same tribal affiliation. Their stories have probably been absorbed into Rabia's biography, leaving us few hard facts about her. The last part of her name, al-Adawiyya, reflects her affiliation with an important branch of the Quraysh tribe, the same branch as that of the Prophet's companion Umar, the second caliph (r. 634–644). Rabia never married, left behind no writings of her own, and no contemporary sources mention her. However, later sources

44

attribute many sayings, poems, and anecdotes to her, highlight-ing her central place among the best-known Muslim Sufis.

Repeatedly biographers have imagined Rabia in a way that suits their message. Sufi hagiographers speak of her as a miracle worker. Several recent writers portray her as model of female independence. One academic writes that "There are as many versions of Rabia's hagiographic persona as there are accounts of her."[3]

Rabia's womanhood seems, if anything, to have augmented her status in Sufi history. And yet the particular difficulties of a woman's experience – and of how she is perceived by men both now and in the past – cannot be discounted. Consider, for exam-ple, Attar's praise of her in his *Memorial of God's Friends*: "A woman who walks on the path of the Lord as ably as a man should not be faulted for being a woman."[4] And the following account illus-trates both her particular challenges and the intense focus of the poems attributed to her:

> Running from a chaser one day, she fell and broke her hand. Humbly prostrating with her face on the ground, she said, "My God, I have no place to go; no parents to turn to; and I am a mere captive with a broken hand. None of this saddens me, because all that concerns me, the only thing I need to know and want to know, is whether you are pleased with me."

As the Quran puts it:

> God's friends should have no fear and no grief
> They have faith and act piously.
> Good tidings await them in worldly life and in the
>   Afterlife.
> The promises of God prevail unaltered, and that is a
>   Supreme Triumph.[5]

Rabia's example demonstrates that a woman could be a friend of God too, without even being a member of the Prophet's household. Revering Rabia emphasizes this possibility, and that being a woman does not rule out the possibility of reaching the highest spiritual rank, just as having the body of a man does not guarantee spiritual superiority. As recorded in hadith, the Prophet Muhammad declares, "God does not regard your forms."

By holding Rabia in highest esteem, Sufism shattered misogynist clichés and opened a space for women's active spiritual presence in the history of Islam.

# 5

# Fatima of Nishapur
## (ca. 1000–1088)

## KEEPER OF THE FAITH

Two hundred years after Rabia, a new chapter opened in the history of Islam, and some of the most exciting developments unfolded in the thriving city of Nishapur, in what is now northeast Iran.

Fatima of Nishapur (ca. 1000–1088) dedicated her long life to commemorating Prophet Muhammad's legacy by recounting his words and deeds, known as hadith. She was born in the city of Nishapur around the year 1000 and died there on the morning of February 9, 1088.

Reports of the sayings and doings of God's messenger set a standard to live up to and a clear path to follow. He treated others kindly and fairly, greeted people with a smile, listened to what they had to say, and always expressed care for everyone – not least for children and women. The collections of hadith report on the way the Prophet prayed in public and in private, what he ate and what he avoided, and his manners and approaches to everything. For example, when asked about drinking, he proclaimed: "Whatever intoxicates you is forbidden." When asked about property, he said, "Whoever revives dead land owns it." To follow the exemplary conduct of the Prophet, which the hadith record, is a religious priority in Islam, next to abiding by the words of God in the Quran.

Fatima lived at a time when a decisive emphasis on hadith learning was developing. The tenth and eleventh centuries witnessed vigorous attempts at identifying authentic hadith. The teaching of hadith has always been taken very seriously. Listeners are virtually transported into the presence of the Prophet to hear what he said. A teacher of hadith, also called a hadith transmitter, links the listeners to the Prophet himself, through a generation-by-generation chain of transmission that ideally goes back to eye-witnesses. Hadith from the past helped make sense of the present and suggested what Muslim men and women were expected to do.

Women also taught hadith. Over the centuries of Islamic history, women have played a fundamental role in the transmission of hadith, primarily to other women. So-called biographical dictionaries contain their names, life-stories and specimens of the hadith that they relayed.[1]

Fatima embodied and exemplified the culture of hadith transmission in her time. Her grandson commemorated her in these words:

> Fatima was the pride of women of her age. She lived in pious submission for ninety years, never busying herself with mundane matters.

Fatima's city of Nishapur was interesting in itself and important in the history of Islam. It lies on a rich strip of agricultural land in northeast Iran. Bounded by tall mountains to the north and a barren desert to the south, this area has long provided a corridor for peoples, armies, merchants and travelers. The town was built by and named after the Zoroastrian King Shapur (r. 240–270 CE) of the Sasanian dynasty of Iran. Earlier a diocese of the Nestorian Christians, Nishapur was conquered by the Muslims, without struggle, during the caliphate of caliph Umar in the seventh century. By the ninth and tenth centuries commercial and other ties connected the city with other centers of Muslim rule as far west as southern Spain and as far east as China.

Under Muslim rule, Nishapur became a major city in Khorasan, a large province that is now divided up between the countries of Iran, Turkmenistan, Afghanistan and Uzbekistan. Khorasan gained in prominence in the eighth century, especially after its Arab and non-Arab inhabitants overthrew the Umayyad dynasts in Damascus and helped establish the Abbasid caliphate in Baghdad. By the middle of the ninth century, Khorasan stood as a practically autonomous province with strong ties to the seat of the caliphate a thousand miles away. Local dynasties ruled as the caliph's vassals, sending him tribute and acknowledging him as the successor to the Prophet. The overwhelming majority of the city's population was Sunni, meaning they upheld strict loyalty to the Abbasid caliph's sovereignty and exclusive reliance on the exemplary conduct of the Prophet, or *sunna*, as the requirements of proper faith.

Hadith transmission became a regular part of the religious life of the Muslim urban elite, including the Nishapuris. At public assemblies and in private sessions, young children would sit at the feet of elder transmitters and listen while accompanying adults took notes on their behalf. There were also *dhikr* sessions: preaching and recounting of moral anecdotes about the life and conduct of the Prophet and his companions. Some groups also practiced the chanting of God's names or recited devotional poetry. We are told that Fatima's father, Abu Ali the Miller, doted on his daughter as he would on a son and took the child to the *dhikr* assemblies of the most renowned teachers in town.

During Fatima's lifetime, Nishapur witnessed major changes in the political and religious history of Islam. General Toghril Beg (ca. 990–1063), who commanded a huge army, entered the city in 1038, taking a decisive step in establishing a huge empire and empowering Islam. Giving a new dynasty of kings the name of their ancestor Seljuk, Toghril Beg and his brother Chaghri Beg (ca. 989–1060) headed the largest ever confederacy of Turkish warriors. The brothers promised to restore the diminished glory of the caliphate, effectively spearheading what has been called a "Sunni Revival."

Nishapur played a big role in the so-called Sunni Revival. Two key institutions in the history of Islam had their roots there: colleges for the study of law, known as madrasas, and the Sufi lodges, or *khaneqahs*. Both underwent decisive changes during Fatima's lifetime. The changes coincided with the rise of the Seljuks and the spread of their authority westward from Khorasan to Iraq and beyond.

A key element of the Sunni Revival was agreeing on a shared conception of the Prophet's exemplary conduct, as revealed by the hadith. By this time countless written collections of hadith had appeared, some containing thousands of sayings. Various schools of thought projected their ideals back to the time of the Prophet. Utilizing paper as a medium for disseminating knowledge, scribes brokered a transition from the memorization of hadith to their preservation in writing. Building on earlier attempts, hadith transmitters in eleventh-century Nishapur, and elsewhere, brought order to the massive collection of hadith. Eventually, they agreed on six major hadith collections, which set exacting standards of soundness and authenticity for canonical (*sahih*) hadith.

Fatima's work focused on two of these six canonical collections of hadith. One had been compiled by Muhammad al-Bukhari (ca. 810–870), originally from the city of Bukhara in present-day Uzbekistan. He had accepted 2,700 hadith out of the 600,000 that he had examined. These numbers are not exact but figurative. The rest he rejected. The result was simply called Bukhari's canonical collection. The other one, compiled by Abu-l-Husayn Muslim of Nishapur (ca. 815–875), was known as Muslim's canonical collection. Muslim's tomb in Nishapur was a place of pilgrimage, where Fatima had probably paid homage.

Although they stood together in opposition to the Shia world view, the Sunnis of Nishapur did not agree on everything. Two major Sunni factions, the Shafiis and the Hanafis, rivaled each other, both named after the eighth-century founders of two distinct frameworks, or *madhab*s, for working out the requirements and implications of Islamic law in personal conduct and communal relations. Various communities, down to the level of city neighborhoods, followed a *madhab* that helped shape its distinct identity. While the *madhab*s are often presented as various schools of law, they can also be seen as recognizable legal communities, or communities molded by certain legal prescriptions.

By the twelfth and thirteenth centuries, four distinct Sunni *madhab*s had taken shape, which would continue until the present. These were the Malikis (located mainly in the western Mediterranean, including Spain); the Shafiis (mainly in South-East Asia and Egypt); the Hanbalis (who would come to dominate Saudi Arabia in the eighteenth century); and the Hanafis (mainly in Turkey and the Arab Middle East). Besides legal differences, for example, on how to divide inherited wealth, the Sunni *ulama* from different *madhab*s also disagreed on theological questions more than other *madhab*s. For example, the Shafiis increasingly emphasized the mystical dimensions of Islam, embracing the legacy of the Sufis of earlier centuries.

Fatima's father, Abu Ali the Miller (ca. 950–1014) was a well-liked and respected Shafii-Sufi. People admired him for his integrity of character, his personal piety, his excellence as an orator and his role as a moral guide. Actively involved in the religious life of his city, he built a *khaneqah* and a madrasa. The same building may have been used for both, probably at different stages of Abu Ali's intellectual life. He aimed to unite the Shafiis of Nishapur around the Sufi ethos, which combines devotion, discipline and acute awareness of God's presence with altruism and compassion for all humans, regardless of their beliefs.

Fatima's greatest teacher was her father. From her childhood, he inculcated in her the love of God and loyalty to the Prophet's legacy. She was only fourteen when he died, but his efforts had set the trajectory for her life. His friend Muhammad al-Sulami (ca. 937–1021) also had a deep and enduring influence on Fatima's intellectual and spiritual life. As a Shafii-Sufi, a hadith transmitter and commentator on the Quran, al-Sulami had acquired a considerable following in Nishapur. Decades before Abu Ali opened his madrasa, al-Sulami had established a small Sufi lodge, with an extensive library that he had inherited from earlier Sufis in the city. Al-Sulami stood as an heir to the Sufi tradition that had emerged in Iraq during the eighth century CE, from the time of Rabia.

Fatima started taking lessons from al-Sulami while her father was still alive. He helped shaped her outlook on the mystical interpretations of the Quran and the proper practice of Sufism. Among dozens of other writings, al-Sulami wrote a biographical treatise on Sufi women. This work testifies that religiously devoted, pious women could often overcome the social and cultural barriers they otherwise faced. Al-Sulami cites examples of early women Sufis who advised their male counterparts, implying that women were on a par with men in matters of the soul.[2] He includes biographies of several women who either lived in Nishapur or practiced their devotions there.

In eleventh-century Nishapur, Sufism opened a space for the fuller participation of women in the religious life of the community. These women played an important role in the process of standardizing hadith transmission, actively choosing which material to teach from canonical works. Most of their students were girls, but boys or even men could attend, listening from behind a curtain. As communal acts of preserving and sharing knowledge, this activity tied in well with the efforts of the male *ulama*. Fatima's father was not alone in initiating his daughter into this culture of religious learning.[3]

Next to her father and his friend al-Sulami, Fatima's husband was also an intellectual and spiritual interlocutor for her.

Abu-l-Qasim al-Qushayri (ca. 986–1074) had been a protégé of both men. When Fatima married him in around 1012, a couple of years before Abu Ali's death, she was about twelve and the groom in his twenties.

On his father's side, Fatima's husband was a Qushayri, a descendant of the Arab clan of Qushayr. Members of the Qushayri clan had settled in the area around Nishapur in the heat of the Arab conquests during the seventh and eighth centuries. By the eleventh century, they had strong business connections inside the city and owned estates outside it. Abu-l-Qasim's mother was descended from another clan of Arab settlers in the region, the Sulamis, the same clan to which their mentor, al-Sulami belonged. Like the Qushayris, the Sulamis and other Arab clans in and around Nishapur had intermarried with local families. They adopted local traditions while still proudly upholding their Arab heritage.

The union of Fatima and Abu-l-Qasim reflected the refashioning of Sufism in Nishapur during the eleventh century. Unlike Fatima, who was born into a scholarly family, Abu-l-Qasim had to assimilate into it. As a youth, he had learned Arabic poetry and rhetoric at home, but mainly he was trained in business matters, horsemanship and military arts. He lacked training in hadith, law, theology or Sufism. One day, during a business trip to Nishapur, he had chanced upon a circle of Sufi devotees of Fatima's father. Welcoming the young man's interest, Abu Ali took him under his wing and introduced him to the best scholarly circles in town.

Al-Qushayri proved himself a worthy apprentice. By his early thirties he was expert in Shafii law and theology and had gained a solid reputation as a Sufi. Two centuries later, an admiring follower wrote of him:

> He was the master of the masters, the teacher of the whole congregation, and the foremost leader of the community who embodied many different kinds of knowledge.

Giving his beloved daughter's hand to al-Qushayri indicates what high hopes Abu Ali had for both of them. He had chosen well. Fatima functioned as a linchpin in a kinship network distinguished by religious learning and piety. Her marriage to al-Qushayri further cemented this role. Together they had at least eight children, most of whom committed themselves to the promotion of Shafii and Sufi ideals. The marriages of their children further extended their scholarly influence. Their daughters, granddaughters and third-generation descendants are known to have intermarried with other important families. Many of them received praise for their pious conduct and their hadith studies. Over seven generations, dozens of Fatima's descendants made a name for themselves.

Fatima's biographers have not attributed any works to her. However, al-Qushayri's copious writings, including his multi-volume commentary on the Quran and his definitive guide to Sufi teachings, may bear traces of Fatima's intellectual influence. The following passage from al-Qushayri's standard treatise on Sufi thought and practice is typical of the ideas Fatima and her husband shared:

> According to Sufi principles, our innermost self embodies and reflects a direct vision of the divine. Much in the same way that the spirit embodies and reflects love and the heart embodies and reflects knowledge. The Sufis say that the innermost self provides a window through which a glimpse of God is revealed.[4]

Fatima's life reflects the culture of eleventh-century Nishapur, where the elite exalted religious learning and piety among women as well as men. This culture welcomed women's religious participation as an element in the broader process of standardizing Sunni Islam.

# 6

# Arwa of Yemen

(ca. 1050–1138)

## THE QUEEN OF SHEBA *REDUX*

While the Sunni Revival was in full swing in Baghdad, Nishapur, and other parts of the Abbasid caliphate, different forms of Shia Islam continued to survive. Some thrived peacefully under Abbasid rule. Others did not. Most notably, upholding the Shia credo, the Fatimid caliphate presented itself as a formidable adversary of the Abbasids. Based in Cairo from the tenth century, it extended its reach as far south as Yemen and as far east as India. A formidable ally of the Fatimids was the longtime female ruler of Yemen, Queen Arwa, whose pomp, power, and prestige reminded people of the famed ancient Queen of Sheba, who is mentioned in the Quran as well as the Bible.

Best known as "the noblewoman" (*Sayyida-al-hurra*), Queen, or *Malika*, Arwa (ca. 1050–1138) was a remarkable sovereign. Like the formidable Queen of Sheba, Arwa ruled Yemen. Neither the first nor the only Muslim woman to rule in Islamic history, still she remains unique in many ways. She enjoyed an exceptionally long reign and widespread recognition of her suzerainty and her authority to rule. She held religious authority as well as political power over a vast domain.

Many Muslim women have ruled, but usually not for long. Sooner rather than later, and more often than not, a strongman rose to seize power and things ended unfavorably for the unseated woman ruler. By contrast, Queen Arwa effectively ruled for six decades. At first she reigned alongside her husband, as other powerful Muslim women before her had had a hand in running state affairs. But after a brief period of joint rule, Arwa's first husband suffered a debilitating illness and in effect she became the *de facto* ruler. When he died she remarried but went on to rule as before. Then her second husband died and after that she continued to rule for more than another fifty years on her own.

Queen Arwa's daily life was typical of a Muslim sovereign's of the time: she held court; minted coins; fought wars; negotiated peace treaties; collected taxes, tribute and other revenues; built cities, mosques and marketplaces; and extended patronage to builders, poets and other exponents of high culture. Her shrine still stands as a site of pilgrimage in the Congregational Mosque that she had built at the center of Jibla – today a thousand-year-old town in the south western highlands of what is now tragically war-ravaged Yemen.

Arwa had lost her father, Ahmad al-Sulayhi, in childhood. She grew up under the care of her uncle, Ali al-Sulayhi (ca. 1010–1067), and his capable consort Asma (ca. 1020–1075). As a prominent member of the Sulayhi clan, Arwa's uncle had forged active alliances with several local tribes and made peace pacts with others. Still others he fought. Combining his skills in negotiation and warfare, by 1047 he had carved out a territory to rule. From his base in the city of Sanaa, he drew on the manpower of close kinsmen and tribal allies to govern an area in Yemen that extended westward to the prosperous town of Zabid and southward to the strategic port of Aden. When Arwa took the reins of power in the 1070s, she continued her uncle's work. By the early twelfth century, her reach went beyond south Yemen. She controlled a network of exchange in goods, ideas and loyalties that spread as far north as what are now Oman, Qatar and Bahrain, and as far eastward as the state of Gujarat in India.

Politically, Sulayhi rule was a branch of the Fatimid Empire. With its capital in the magnificent city of Cairo, the Fatimid Empire had strong allies throughout Muslim lands. Its reach stretched beyond its base in Egypt and North Africa to Sicily, Iraq, Arabia, Iran, Tajikistan, even as far as India. The Sulayhi enterprise that Arwa's uncle had initiated successfully united pro-Fatimid political forces in eleventh-century Yemen.

Throughout Arwa's lifetime, two major political dynasties competed for the leadership of the world's large Muslim populace, the *umma*. Both claimed to be caliphates, or legitimate heirs to the political tradition that Prophet Muhammad had established. One was the Abbasids in Baghdad, the other the Fatimids in Cairo. A close third contender, the Umayyad caliphate in Córdoba, had lost its grip on power several years before Arwa's birth. The Abbasids and the Fatimids competed against each other politically, militarily, economically and ideologically.

The Abbasids had built Baghdad shortly after the triumph of the so-called Abbasid revolution in the middle of the eighth century. Although the Fatimids had established themselves in Cairo a couple of centuries later, they too had quickly risen to the height of caliphal grandeur. Both caliphates ruled in the name of Islam and both supported Islamic institutions. They founded and funded mosques, upheld and enacted Muslim rites, and extended patronage to men of learning, known as the *ulama*.

The fundamental difference between the two dynasties was that the Abbasids were Sunni and the Fatimids Shia. Every single Abbasid and Fatimid caliph denigrated his rival as an imposter and proclaimed himself the rightful successor of Prophet Muhammad. Each claimed exclusively for himself the title of Commander of the Faithful, *amir-al-muminin*. This was not merely personal. The two caliphates legitimized religious authority on different grounds.

The Abbasid caliphs presented themselves as custodians of Sunni Islam. With their endorsement, the *ulama* had articulated the various tenets of Muslim theology and had sought to codify Prophet Muhammad's exemplary conduct, or *sunna*, in detail. Sometimes referred to as the sharia, the interpretation of this elaborate code of conduct formed the basis of Islamic law.

Under the Abbasids, the *ulama* drew on their expertise to mobilize social forces around them. Mindful of the variety of positions, regional variations, and preferences in legal thinking and practice, the Abbasid caliphate officially recognized as many as four distinct frameworks for the interpretation of the sharia. These are known as the standard Sunni schools of law, or *madhab*s: the Hanafi, Shafii, Maliki and Hanbali, each named after its founder.

The Fatimids advocated a different principle. They called for obedience to a living, personal embodiment of Prophet Muhammad's divinely ordained authority. For the Fatimids, this could be none other than the Fatimid caliph. The Fatimids claimed to descend from Prophet Muhammad through his revered daughter Fatima, and named themselves accordingly.

Contrary to the Abbasid view, the Fatimid caliph combined in himself political as well as religious authority. In principle, he was the Imam as well as the caliph. Therefore, living by his infallible commands took precedence over any fallible attempts at codifying and interpreting the sharia.

There existed other Shias outside the Fatimid realm as well. Shias who remained loyal to the Abbasids and their allies everywhere renounced the Fatimid Imam-caliphs. The elite of the Shia community in eleventh-century Baghdad even signed a document that dismissed the Fatimid claim of descent from the Prophet's daughter. Instead, the majority of Shias in Baghdad, Kufa, Basra, and in such Iranian cities as Qum and Nishapur adopted a radically different alternative. To them, the rightful heir of Ali and Fatima, the true Imam, had disappeared from public eye. He was to return only at the end of time, and no one could foretell when that would be. The political stakes tied to the theological position were high.

In Yemen, Arwa's uncle targeted the political authority of the Abbasid caliphate as well as the authority of the local Sunni *ulama*. Before that, the Sulayhi clan had followed the Sunni Shafii *madhab*. Arwa's uncle spearheaded his campaign in the name of the pro-Fatimid "Campaign for Guidance." A shift in religious preference mirrored a shift in political loyalty, and vice versa.

Women participated in the Campaign for Guidance. Arwa and her mother-in-law, Asma, played active roles in it along with Arwa's uncle, her first husband, and probably her second husband as well. In an official decree dated 1089, the incumbent Fatimid caliph appointed Queen Arwa to supervise the Campaign for Guidance in India directly. Earlier, she had informed the caliph in writing that the previous overseer of the campaign there had died and that his son pursued commercial interests to the detriment of campaign-related duties.

Ideologically, the Fatimid claim to legitimacy derived from a woman, albeit an extraordinary one – Fatima, daughter of Khadija and Prophet Muhammad (see Chapter 2). Even Ali, the most revered man after Prophet Muhammad in the Shia world view, received praise for being her husband, besides many other merits of his own. The engraving on the gold coins, or *dinars*, minted as early as the middle of the tenth century by a powerful Fatimid caliph read:

Ali is the Prophet's Nominee, the Most Excellent Representative, the Husband of the Radiant Chaste One.

Here the epithet "Radiant Chaste One" refers to Fatima.

Although explicit reference to a woman on coinage remained exceptional, a practice of issuing coins to commemorate Fatima's birth, death, and marriage continued. Such coins capitalized on the Fatimid caliphate's claim to a revered lineage. Also, the name of Fatima was included in the blessing formula adopted by the Fatimids for recitation at the start of every public sermon (*khutba*) in Friday congregational prayers:

> Praise be on Muhammad, on Ali and on Fatima the chaste, on al-Hasan and al-Husayn, and on the Imams, forefathers of the chief commander of believers.

Fatimid approval of Queen Arwa's reign in Yemen reflected the Fatimid caliphate's openness to women's activity in politics. Their strong support for a woman ruler contrasted sharply with the policies and practices of the rival Abbasid caliphate. Under the Abbasids, women of the court figured as mothers, daughters, daughters-in-law, sisters, wives, wet-nurses, and concubines. Through political matchmaking, suitable women often served as tokens of loyalty. Sometimes they urged on powerful men's decisions. Wealthy women made endowments for the building of mosques and funded other pious undertakings. But that was all. By contrast, Fatimid women played these roles – but also others. For a couple of years during the 1020s, a royal woman practically ran the Fatimid Empire. The caliphate's subjects regularly petitioned royal women, not only asking them for money but also beseeching them to intercede in political matters on their behalf. In some cases, women signed and sent political and diplomatic documents.

Arwa and her mother-in-law, Asma, corresponded with the Fatimid caliph and the royal women of the court in Cairo. Many of the letters were simply official, but others were personal, marking moments of daily joy or grief, announcing births, deaths, and marriages. The caliph himself dispatched a signed and sealed letter to congratulate Arwa when she gave birth to her son.

When Arwa's husband died in 1064, the daughter of a previous caliph sent her a letter of condolence. Acknowledging the living caliph's recognition of Arwa's son as the rightful ruler of Yemen, she asserted that the members of the ruling clan, as well as all the believers in Yemen, ought to remain loyal to Queen Arwa and her son. That son died soon after the murder of Arwa's uncle. Shortly after that, in a letter dated 1069, the ruling caliph's consort praised Arwa's role in advancing the goals of the Campaign for Guidance in her realm. Twenty years later, the same caliph placed Arwa in charge of Fatimid interests in India. In her letter, the caliph's consort expressed her expectation of seeing the Yemeni queen support her son's succession to the caliphate. At the appropriate time, Queen Arwa weighed in favorably on his behalf.

That was in 1094, when disputes over succession tore the Fatimids apart. Battles broke out here and there. Turmoil inside the court and divisions in society were compounded by the outbreak of an unprecedented military confrontation with non-Muslim armies: the Crusaders.

Launched at the turn of the twelfth century, the massive mobilization of Christian troops, known as the Crusades, set in motion a train of world-changing events. The First Crusade, that began in 1095, culminated in the capture of Jerusalem from its Muslim rulers in July 1099. Armies of the Cross put the city's Muslim and Jewish inhabitants to the sword and established the Christian Kingdom of Jerusalem.

As a result of the battles over the Fatimid succession, hardship forced even court women to trade their jewelry for food. Some turned to begging on the streets of Cairo. The grotesque report in some sources that "plump-legged women were eaten alive" may have been a mere rumor. But possibly not!

The two major contending parties were named after their choice of the caliph: the supporters of Nizar versus the supporters of Mustali. Queen Arwa joined the chorus of other Fatimid women in support of Mustali's claim to the throne. Under her influence the number of Mustali's supporters increased, stretching beyond Cairo all the way from Yemen and Oman to Gujarat in India. She lived up to the expectation that Mustali's mother had expressed by letter decades earlier.

Unlike Yemen, other major outposts of Fatimid sovereignty took Nizar's side. Moving away from Mustali's strongholds in Egypt, Nizar's supporters took to the highlands, in what is now primarily Lebanon, Syria, Jordan, and as far east as Iran and Tajikistan. Alternative formulations of the Campaign for Guidance took shape, independent from Cairo in doctrine, organization and politics. Over time, the divide between them broke up the integrity of the Fatimid caliphate. Some of Nizar's supporters even joined forces with Christian Crusaders to ravage Mustali-supporting villages in and around Antioch, Ascalon, and Jerusalem, though the Crusades did not affect Yemen directly.

Queen Arwa maintained peace in Yemen. She preferred diplomacy over warfare, even as recurrent tribal revolts threatened her hold on important cities and fortresses. She proved herself capable of fighting when necessary, exacting cold-blooded revenge against the west Yemeni tribe that had murdered her uncle and other members of her clan, but Arwa's skill in diplomacy was of far greater importance. Combining religious proselytizing and alliance building with long-distance trade and commercial profit sharing, she spread Islam and Fatimid interests in the Indian Ocean basin. Her allies prospered in Yemen, Oman, and India at the turn of the twelfth century, and in gratitude her subjects sang her praises. At the end of Friday prayers and religious festivals, preachers acknowledged her authority by referring to her by name, along with the Fatimid caliph. Chroniclers who recorded Queen Arwa's accomplishments and circumstances testified that under her, justice prevailed, crops abounded, trade flourished and the people prospered. Some describe her as beautiful, with black eyes and dark skin, but in the absence of any concrete descriptions, it is hard to speculate.

When Queen Arwa died in 1138, Fatimid rule in Yemen ended abruptly. A group of the *ulama* rebelled and quickly seized the fortress from which she had ruled. Politically, they looked up to the Abbasid caliphate in Baghdad. Doctrinally, they were

Sunnis, following the Shafii school of law. The rebellious Shafii *ulama* of twelfth-century Yemen thwarted Fatimid suzerainty, Sulayhid rule, and Shia teachings, all in the same breath. They wished to see in Yemen a similar form of Sunni revival and Shafii empowerment to that which the Seljuks had spearheaded all the way from Uzbekistan to Syria.

To express their disdain for Queen Arwa's legacy, they put on a show. According to an eyewitness report, the Shafii *ulama* ordered the women of the fortress put on colorful clothes and go out on the roof to play tambourines and dance to music. In the world view of the *ulama* and their followers, respectable women do not dance in public view. So, making such a public spectacle was meant as a vilification of Arwa's rule and a public humiliation of the Sulayhids. Within years, communities of faith that she had cultivated from Yemen all the way to India withered.

The Fatimid caliphate was itself teetering on the edge and it, too, collapsed in 1171. The Kurdish general Saladin (ca. 1138–1193) often gets credit for delivering the final blows to both the Fatimids and the Crusaders. With the Fatimids out of the picture, the Abbasid caliphate enjoyed a half-century of unrivaled, though unstable, power. They continued the policy of subverting whatever the Fatimids had upheld, including giving political power to women.

Although historical sources that deal with the role of women in the Fatimid caliphate and its outposts remain few and far between, the example of Malika Arwa shows that female political and religious authority has long been acknowledged in the history of Islam.

Today the embattled people of Yemen fondly remember Queen Arwa as a daughter of their land, a great ruler, and a worthy successor to the legendary queen of Sheba.

# 7

# Terken Khatun

## (ca. 1205–1281)

## DOING WELL AND DOING GOOD

The thirteenth century marks a turning point in the history of Islam, witnessing the coming of the Mongols from the east, the collapse of the Abbasid caliphate, and the massive destruction of many centers of urban life. At the time, a female ruler managed not only to keep her subjects safe but also to bring prosperity to the lands she ruled in what is now southern Iran.

We know her by her title Terken (or Turkan) Khatun. In the Turkic vernacular she spoke, this means noblewoman or princess. Her birth name and exact date or place of birth remain unknown. Sources tell us that she had been captured into slavery as a child, somewhere near western China, perhaps in Xinjiang (Chinese Turkistan), sometime around 1210 CE. So we may surmise that she came from a newly Muslim or even non-Muslim lineage, probably Buddhist. However, she grew up as a Muslim and later distinguished herself as a paragon of charity and patron of Islamic learning.

At the time that Terken Khatun was captured into slavery, armies of the Muslim rulers of the Kharazmshahi dynasty were raiding the lands on the north western border of China. She was probably taken by the slave drivers who often followed behind armies. By chance she soon found herself in the house of a merchant in the city of Isfahan, central Iran. He adopted her as a step-daughter and spared no expense on educating her. She was a bright and attractive girl and he had high hopes for her, perhaps for marriage to a prince in his town. However, the town's judge, or *qadi*, tried to coerce the merchant and take Terken Khatun away from him. The merchant complained to Ghiyas-al-Din Kharazmshah, a member of the Kharazmshahi dynasty, who was passing through Isfahan on an expedition. To solve the problem, the prince took the merchant's adoptive daughter away from him and made her his own wife. A local history written in the four-teenth century reports that the Isfahani merchant reacted by saying, "I thought you had rescued me from a wolf, but as I looked closer, I saw you *are* the wolf."

Far more devastating horrors followed for the merchant, for Terken Khatun, and for the world. The thirteenth century witnessed the coming of the Mongols from the east, a prolonged invasion that rooted out or disrupted the customary ways of Muslim societies.

The Mongols came in waves. First came Genghis Khan (ca. 1162–1227), the warlord who had united Mongol tribesmen at the turn of the thirteenth century. He led his horsemen into Muslim lands, sweeping all the way from the towns of Samarkand and Bukhara in what is now Uzbekistan, to Herat in Afghanistan and Nishapur in Iran. Under his command, the Mongols razed cities, burned crops and killed people, laying swathes of land to waste. The hometown of Fatima of Nishapur was no more. Contemporary sources claim that the Mongols killed hundreds of thousands of people and razed dozens of cities to the ground. Modern scholarship questions these numbers, suggesting that the Mongols themselves had a stake in having their power exagger-ated and thereby instilling fear in the hearts of their enemies as well as their own subjects. The undeniable reality is that to

Muslim onlookers the Mongols appeared like God-sent damnation.

Genghis returned to Mongolia by about 1222, leaving behind vassal rulers here and there. One of those Mongol vassalages took shape that same year in Kerman, a desert city in south east Iran with easy access to the port of Hormuz on the Persian Gulf and the Sea of Oman. The new ruler of Kerman, Baraq or Buraq, fancied himself as a consummate go-between and dealmaker. As a gesture of loyalty, he had married one of his daughters to Genghis Khan's second son Chagatai Khan (1183–1242). He also sent tribute to Baghdad, deferring to the caliph's authority as his Muslim suzerain. At the same time, he became close to the Kharamzshahis. Baraq kept all channels open, making sure that whoever was in power saw him as an ally. However, because of the insecurity of his political maneuverings, Baraq showed no mercy to potential rivals. So when opportunity presented itself, he murdered Ghiyas-al-Din Kharazmshah, who was staying in Kerman as his guest. At the time, 1228, Terken Khatun was staying at a friend's house in the nearby city of Yazd. Having killed her first husband, Baraq forcibly brought Terken Khatun to Kerman, claiming her as his own possession, referring to Genghis's Decrees, known as the Great *Yasa*. Baraq died a few years later, in 1235. Once again Terken Khatun had to safeguard her place, not to mention save her life, by making new arrangements, first with the dead man's heirs, and, more importantly, with their Mongol overlords.

She married Baraq's nephew and heir-apparent. However, succession arrangements changed under pressure from the local dynasty's Mongol overlords, and a son of the previous ruler ascended to the throne in Kerman. Terken Khatun and her new husband left town in 1236 and spent the next sixteen years and seven months in the eastern parts of the Mongol Empire, mostly in or around China.

Ogedei Khan (ca. 1185–1241), the third son and successor of Genghis Khan, received the couple with courtesy. In those years, he was preoccupied with extending Mongol rule over large parts of China and Korea. Upon her husband's death, his wife Toregene Khatun (d. 1246) succeeded him, ruling for five years as her minor son's regent. Toregene liked Terken Khatun and with her support, the position of Terken Khatun and her husband improved in the Mongol court, to the extent that when Mongke Khan (1209–1259) took over as the next great Khan or Khaqan of the Mongol Empire in 1251, he appointed Terken Khatun's husband to rule over Kerman. Terken Khatun rode at her husband's side as they entered the city in 1252.

In 1255 Genghis Khan's grandson Hulegu Khan (ca. 1218–1265) launched the second major wave of Mongol invasions. Three decades after his grandfather had returned to Mongolia, Hulegu came back to wreak havoc again in Muslim lands and to stay much longer. Because the Mongol warlord and his troops were not Muslims, they offered no preferential treatment to the different Muslim groups or sects they encountered. They torched villages, wrecked irrigation systems, sacked cities and turned mosques into stables without discrimination. In eastern and north-central Iran, the Mongols destroyed the forts of once pro-Fatimid Ismaili Shias, Nizaris, who had fought against the Abbasid caliphate and its local Sunni allies for over a century. Pushing his way to Baghdad, Hulegu had the Abbasid caliph killed in 1258, thus removing the last vestiges of unified Muslim rule from the once glorious City of Peace that the Abbasids had built half a millennium earlier. Baghdad's downfall left a gap in the collective memory of Muslims, a gap as big, or as small, as the notion of the caliphate.

Terken Khatun's husband, who was a capable general himself, had joined the armies of Hulegu as of June 1256. However, he fell ill and had to return to Kerman, where he died in September 1257. Yet again Terken Khatun had to act quickly. She sent envoys to Hulegu Khan's military camp (the *ordo*). She requested to be allowed to continue to rule Kerman as her minor son's rightful regent. On his way to Baghdad, the Mongol warlord ordered a power-sharing arrangement. Terken Khatun should rule over administrative and fiscal matters while her husband's son-in-law commanded the army. Wanting the ruling changed, Terken Khatun left Kerman for an audience with Hulegu. She argued that she would be a better ruler for Kerman, and a better ally for the Mongols, if she had full power. He agreed.

Terken Khatun took over as sovereign in 1258. A contemporary local history of Kerman describes her as follows:

> She was a queen, with an auspicious shadow of the loftiest rank, who conducted herself chastely and demurely, ruled with justice, decency, and high moral qualities. Her reign was strong and her days were days of propriety . . . As a sovereign she resembled the Queen of Sheba and in purity she followed in the path of Rabia.

During the years of hardship when most neighboring lands were in chaos, Terken Khatun brought increased prosperity to Kerman. To strengthen her ties to the Mongols, she arranged for her son to marry a Mongol princess, a daughter of Arghun. Years later, in 1271, she gave her own sixteen-year-old daughter, Padshah Khatun, as a bride to Hulegu's son Abaqa Khan (r. 1265–1282), who held sovereignty over the southern and western parts of the Mongol Empire, extending from Afghanistan to parts of present-day Turkey. Like her mother, Padshah Khatun was known for her beauty. At the time beautiful meant looking Chinese or Turkic. The lyrical literature of the thirteenth century strongly reflects this aesthetic preference: almond eyes, a small nose, tiny lips, and ruddy cheeks on a flat face. When her daughter was a child, Terken Khatun put boys' clothing on her to divert any inappropriate attention from the men of her court.

Soon Kerman's economy boomed, with agriculture growing and the city thriving as a center of textile trade. Terken Khatun spent the incoming wealth on the city itself. Charitable endow-ments and public institutions upheld her rule; known as *oqaf* in Islamic law, such endowments have always provided a means of controlling wealth by dedicating it to religiously acceptable causes. Either directly or indirectly, Terken Khatun started all the major charitable endowments in Kerman during the thir-teenth century. Her generosity seemed boundless.

Although at the time the Ilkhans, the Mongol rulers of the Ilkhanate, were not yet Muslim, under Terken Khatun, Kerman flourished as a center of Islamic learning. She rebuilt and expanded the madrasa that her husband had founded in Kerman. Three days every week she would visit the site of the building, supervising the progress of the work. She earmarked revenues from multiple fruit gardens and agricultural lands for use at the madrasa, keeping the space well-lit at night, employing teachers, and paying stipends to students. According to a surviving deed of endowment, she had the equivalent of 720 *man*s (a unit of weight roughly equal to 3–5 kilo-grams) of wheat paid to the male servants at the madrasa and the equivalent of 500 *man*s of wheat to the female servants. For centu-ries, the madrasa carried her title—the Madrasa of the Chaste Lady.

Terken Khatun brought a high-profile teacher to the madrasa. However, the man betrayed her trust. He allied himself with Terken Khatun's local rivals, including her son, who was disgrun-tled at not having more power for himself. The madrasa instruc-tor went as far as accusing Terken Khatun of unchaste and unbecoming conduct. Islamic law does not take such an accusa-tion lightly. Chastising Aisha's accusers, the Quran itself was explicit on this: "Anyone who accuses chaste women but fails to bring forth four witnesses then flog them eighty strikes. And reject their testimony ever after, for those are wicked transgressors."[1] There was no backing for such a claim against a ruling queen. Terken Khatun did not flog her accuser, she simply cut off his stipend and removed him from his teaching position. Being a woman was not easy, even for a queen.

The hospital she built in 1261 similarly drew on massive endowed revenues. The appointed master physician received the equivalent of 5000 *man*s of wheat in stipends every year. The hospital's manager received 2000, the inhouse apothecary 1000, and each of the three employees of the hospital 700 *man*s of wheat per annum.

Terken Khatun had a hand in running the affairs of Kerman for over forty years. She too was favorably compared to the Queen of Sheba. After a period of instability in Kerman, Terken Khatun's daughter, Padshah Khatun, succeeded her on the throne. Padshah reigned briefly, focusing on preserving the charitable endowments her mother had established. The instructor her mother had hired and then dismissed issued a *fatwa* to nullify all the endowments she had made. He contended that Terken Khatun was not pious enough to have such endowments in her name. Padshah Khatun brought in another scholar to teach in her mother's madrasa, who gladly voided that *fatwa*.

However, with Terken Khatun's demise a golden age in Kerman drew to a close. She kept her city safe and prosperous during a very difficult time. Her legacy lives on, especially in the memory of the thousands of girls and women who have attended schools named after her in Kerman.

# 8

# Shajara'-al-Durr
## (d. 1257)

### PERILS OF POWER, BETWEEN
### CALIPHS AND MAMLUKS

During the thirteenth century, ravening Mongol armies wreaked havoc in Muslim lands, with a few exceptions such as Kerman. However, they failed to move beyond Egypt. The Mamluk commanders of Egypt halted their relentless advance, decisively defeating them in 1260 at the Battle of Ayn-Jalut, or Goliath's Spring, in south eastern Galilee.

Mamluk generals had taken full charge of Egypt just a few years earlier. Their rise to dominance partly stemmed from the plight of an outstanding young woman we shall refer to as Shajara. At a time when military pressure from the outside and internal discord threatened the fabric of Muslim society in Cairo, Shajara brought her outstanding talents into play, tackling multiple crises as a politician and a leader, while still carrying out the duties of a wife and mother.

Shajara started out as a slave-girl, or concubine. Her origins, even her birth name, remain unknown to us. Her earliest mention appears in the annals of the year 1239, listing her among many other slave-girls in the women's quarter, or harem, of the Abbasid caliph. She was probably born not long before

1230. Some say she hailed from an Armenian, therefore Christian, background. Others say she was a Turk, therefore Muslim-born. She was about eleven when the caliph sent her from Baghdad to either Damascus or Cairo, as a gift for the young Prince Salih al-Aiyubi (ca. 1225–1249) of the Aiyubid princely house. A concubine was regarded as an appropriate gift to send an ally at the time.

Members of the Aiyubid dynasty had ruled on behalf of the Abbasid caliphate in parts of the Levant for three generations – a large area that included Egypt, Syria-Palestine, Jordan and some eastern Mediterranean islands. After defeating the Crusaders and recapturing Jerusalem in the name of the Abbasid caliphate, the renowned Kurdish general Saladin had founded the Aiyubid dynasty, naming it in honor of his ancestor Aiyub, who had become a Muslim sometime in the tenth or eleventh century.

The Aiyubid prince Salih put a name on the caliph's present. He called her Shajara'al-Durr—Pearl Tree, Tree of Pearls or, as one translator has rendered it, Spray-of-Pearls.[1] She had other titles and names as well, but it is perhaps easiest to call her simply Shajara. The prince's choice of name for the young woman indicates how much he valued her presence in his life. She won Salih's love and trust with her dedication and loyalty, especially in times of hardship. When a rival Aiyubid cousin banished Salih to the Fortress of Kerak around 1247, Shajara was the only woman who accompanied him into exile. The Crusaders had built this impenetrable maze of stone-vaulted corridors in the twelfth century to safeguard their treasures. It still stands in Jordan, now a tourist attraction. During the years of exile there, Prince Salih only had two companions, Shajara and a strong male Turkic slave called Baibars.

Showing his appreciation, Salih took Shajara as his permanent wife. No longer a mere concubine, she gave him a son and heir, whom they named Khalil. As if the boy had brought them good fortune, within a year the tide turned in their favor and the couple moved to Cairo, the main seat of Aiyubid power. Shajara's husband was now king.

Crisis soon followed. News arrived in the summer of 1249 of yet another clash between Christian invaders and Muslims in the Levant. The Crusaders had seized the port of Damietta in the north and were advancing down the Nile toward Cairo. Shajara's husband had to fight them. What church historians have glorified as the Crusades were, in the eyes of local chroniclers, nothing more than savage acts of banditry by marauders coming from the west.

Some say that the Crusades marked the beginning of western Europe's dominance worldwide. However, at the time the path to European supremacy seemed far from either smooth or guaranteed. In 1187 Muslim armies retook Jerusalem and the Aiyubid general Saladin expelled thousands of Christians who had been settled in the holy city for almost ninety years. Replacing the Crusaders, the Aiyubids extended their power across the region.

Saladin had defined Aiyubid policies around two principal concerns: fighting off the Christian Crusaders and promoting Sunni Islam against the Fatimid Shia caliphate in the Levant. By 1171, he had effectively dethroned the Fatimids; had the Abbasid caliph acknowledged as the Muslim sovereign in the sermon or *khutba* accompanying congregational prayers every Friday; appointed Sunni judges; and supported Sunni institutions, especially in Cairo, Damascus and Jerusalem. For centuries, the legal instrument known in Islamic law as pious endowment (*waqf*) helped legitimize rulers as patrons of learning and moral virtue. Saladin used this instrument strategically. Several Sunni madrasas and Sufi centers (or *khaneqahs*) in Aiyubid territories depended on revenues derived from endowments that he and his descendants made. Sometimes, rather than shouldering the costs of construction, Saladin had Armenian and Latin Christian buildings seized and converted for Muslim use.

After Saladin died in 1193, Jerusalem changed hands a few times. In 1248, King Louis IX of France (r. 1226–1270) declared a new campaign to wrest the holy city from the Aiyubids. Setting sail across the Mediterranean from southern France, he set foot on Egyptian soil before continuing to his destination. He had timed his attack to take advantage of reports about the Muslim ruler's debilitating sickness. Salih offered the French king an opportunity to negotiate. Rebuffed, Salih went to war, transported in a litter because his illness prevented him from riding a horse. Again, in that cold fall, Shajara accompanied him.

Salih died of severe tuberculosis on the move to ward off the crusaders. He was forty-four. His young widow knew that when a king died, his men often rebelled, disbanded or even joined the enemy's side. Could Aiyubid rule continue? Shajara had to fight to secure her own life and the future of Khalil, the son she had had with her deceased husband. What could she do to maintain the army's morale? She improvised. She sent notice to Salih's heir-apparent, Turanshah, urging him to rush to her side. Meanwhile, she concealed the king's death. She cut all access to the dead man's chamber. She continued taking meals there herself, behaving as if nothing had changed. The Lebanese French author Amin Maalouf provides an engaging account of what happened, in his popular book *The Crusades Through Arab Eyes*.

Waiting for Turanshah to arrive, Shajara ruled. The annual flooding of the Nile, which did not significantly subside until November, helped in keeping the Crusaders at bay. Meanwhile, she relied on two co-conspirators – her husband's right-hand man in the army and her eunuch at the court. As the king's consort, she routinely communicated her wishes and commands through eunuchs, who were considered neither male nor female and therefore served as appropriate go-betweens. Now Shajara issued decrees in the name of Salih and had the eunuch sign them in his name. With proper documents in hand, she placed her other ally in command of the army. Her plan worked.

Maalouf, in *The Crusades Through Arab Eyes*, celebrates Shajara as a "providential personality."[2] Thanks to her handling of a potentially disastrous threat, the Aiyubids retained their sovereignty, at least for the time being. Louis returned home, ironically to another strong woman, his own mother Blanche of Castile (1188–1252), who ruled France during his absence.

The problem with conspiracies, even successful ones, is that they often get out of hand. Providential or not, Shajara's role quickly took a turn into uncharted territory. Having routed the crusaders, her deceased husband's generals coveted greater power in running the affairs of state. They opposed the heir-apparent. As they saw it, the man claimed credit for a momentous victory that he owed to them. They protested that Turanshah privileged his own troops over those from Cairo. The Aiyubid claimant failed to push back effectively and a handful of soldiers killed him in 1250. Ready and willing to make the best of a grim situation, Shajara struck a deal with the army's leadership. Showering favors and appointments on them, she convinced the generals to remain obedient to her. Doing so meant that, despite appearances, they had not revolted against the Aiyubids and thus against the Abbasid caliphate. Accepting Shajara's suzerainty would allow them to mitigate the murder of Turanshah. Rather than as a renegade act of violence, they could defend, even legitimate, what had happened as displaying loyalty toward the wife and child of their deceased Aiyubid liege. The generals even took a step further and elevated Shajara to the throne. Reverentially referring to her as Umm Khalil, mother of Khalil, they acknowledged her as their female sovereign, or Sultana. This gesture signaled their unbroken allegiance to the Aiyubid dynasty and thereby to the Abbasid caliphate.

As the reigning queen of Egypt, Shajara proved her mettle, regaining Damietta, liquidating the holdings of the Crusaders in Egypt, and ransoming their captives. Soon, she had a royal seal, with the inscription "Umm Khalil." She minted coins in her own name, and at every Friday congregational prayer, Sunni preachers acknowledged her authority in their sermons. During Shajara's reign, Egypt remained peaceful and stable.

Still, the Abbasid caliph al-Mustasim (r. 1242–1258) objected. Had Shajara crossed a line? Maybe the caliph cringed at seeing a former slave-girl from his father's harem wield so much authority so well. Perhaps the Sunni *ulama* of Baghdad reminded him of the hadith that we saw the companion Abu Bakra had recalled in Basra centuries earlier to condemn Aisha's involvement in the Battle of the Camel: "Succumbing to women's rule is bound to result in decadence." Whatever rationale these exponents of male patriarchy may have used to undermine Shajara at the time, they saw in her a threat that they had to neutralize at once.

Politically as well as legally, the Abbasid caliph in Baghdad held absolute authority over Muslim warriors who wielded their sword in his name, including the Aiyubids and their generals. Those who failed to obey the caliph were not regarded as kings and legitimate warriors but mere unruly warlords and renegade bandits. Even the mightiest and haughtiest general belonged to the caliph, literally like a slave – or *mamluk*. Unlike slaves in the common sense, Mamluks in principle could and often did possess immense power and incredible wealth. Still, regardless of how much they had, the Mamluks owed loyalty and obedience to the caliph.

The Abbasid caliph al-Mustasim threatened the Mamluks in Egypt, ordering them to remove Shajara from the throne or else he would send a new sultan to rule over them. To avert this crisis, Shajara found a way out. She abdicated her position and married one of the Mamluk generals. This man, named Aybek, would be the new general-in-chief. To reconstruct Shajara's possible line of reasoning, first, this gave her a chance to prove her continued allegiance to the caliphate; second, transferring Aiyubid legitimacy to her new husband would safeguard her son's right to the throne; and third, she would still exert influence on matters of importance, as she had during her first husband's reign. Shajara's abdication took effect on July 30, 1250. She had ruled in her own name for only eighty days – less than three months.

Revisiting the exceptional case of Shajara, the Moroccan sociologist Fatima Mernissi (1940–2015) criticizes the Egyptian queen for yielding to the caliph's demand too easily. In her *Forgotten Queens of Islam* (1993), Mernissi condemns what she characterizes as a pathetic act of weakness, a desperate attempt on Shajara's part to gain the caliph's good will by giving up the throne.[3] Mernissi suggests that Shajara ought to have resisted, remembering the results she had achieved a few months earlier by tacitly agreeing to the elimination of Turanshah and then reaping the benefits of his murder. But is this a fair assessment? A closer examination of the tenuous relations between the Mamluks and the caliph, and the cut-throat rivalries in their own ranks, reveals a complicated situation.

When Salih died, Shajara allied herself with a group of Mamluks that remained loyal to her deceased husband's legacy and therefore to herself and her son, Khalil. After that, she relied on her deceased husband's comrades in arms, especially on the formidable warrior Baibars. She had known him since her days of exile alongside Salih in the Fortress of Kerak. Baibars detested Aybek and his band of fellow Mamluks. Having satisfied the caliph by taking the hand of his favored choice, Shajara continued to influence the course of affairs by leaning on her old Mamluk allies who did all in their power to undermine Aybek. The fact that her new husband often had to leave on military campaigns allowed Shajara to exercise *de facto* rule over Egypt during his intermittent periods of absence. Even when he was at home, the former Sultana wielded power behind the scenes.

Tensions remained high in the marriage from its beginning in 1250 to its bloody end in 1257. Shajara refused to divulge the location of Aiyubid treasures to Aybek, who in turn mistreated her. He tried hard, but failed, to erode her power base among the

Mamluks. Still, to undercut Shajara entirely, Aybek sought to bring new women into his harem, not only to hurt her emotionally but also to establish strong nuptial ties with local tribal chieftains who could help uproot those Mamluks who opposed him. Aybek also claimed that he ruled on behalf of a six-year-old prince from the Aiyubid house whose right to the throne took precedence over Khalil, Shajara's son.

Shajara's fortunes unravelled rapidly. According to the medieval chronicles, she lost control when she discovered Aybek's plan to marry another woman. This may be another instance of oversimplification on the part of medieval chroniclers. They say that was why she had her second husband killed. Spicing up their reductive narrative, they describe how a rage-blinded Shajara lured him into her steam bath, or *hammam*. Her eunuchs beat him to death while she rubbed soap into his eyes. Continuing the story, chronicles tell us that within days, Shajara was arrested and delivered to her archnemesis, Aybek's first wife. The angry woman had her killed and ordered her dead body to be thrown over the castle's ramparts. Stray dogs in the streets of Cairo devoured Shajara's body.

Beyond the hackneyed tropes of "Woman beware woman" and "Hell has no fury like a woman scorned," we should note that Shajara was a consummate political player. To claim, as some historians have, that the Mamluks used her as a pawn against their competitors for the Egyptian throne is similarly simplistic. Shajara lived only twenty-eight years or so. During her short life, she collaborated or colluded with some to the detriment of others. She won a few hands, but finally lost the gamble and her life. Her death marks the end of the Aiyubid dynasty.

Historically, Shajara connects Aiyubid and Mamluk rule in Egypt. Mongol armies entered Baghdad in 1258, killed the caliph and put an end to the Abbasid caliphate. Shajara's short life and tragic end made room for the rise of the Mamluks, not merely as warriors but as a redoubtable political force. Some say that in the end the man who dealt the final blow and killed Shajara was none other than Baibars, once her ally, who distinguished himself as the founder of independent Mamluk rule in the Levant.

Shajara's accomplishments, as detailed in the historical annals, have inspired various observers of history to tailor their depictions of her to their particular priorities. Arab nationalists of the 1960s regarded her as a beacon for political independence. Feminist writers continue to look to her as an example of a strong woman leader from medieval times.

*This illustration is based upon an artist's rendering*

# 9

# Sayyida al-Hurra of Tétouan
## (ca. 1492–ca. 1560)

### THE FREE QUEEN

Ageneration after the tide of Mongol invasions subsided in the east, new waves of attacks on Muslims gained momentum in the western parts of the Mediterranean Sea and in Iberia.

In 2017, the United Nations Educational and Cultural Organization (UNESCO) added the Mediterranean port of Tétouan to its Creative Cities Network worldwide,[1] recognizing the traditions of craftsmanship and music in this northwest Moroccan city of almost 400,000 people. Tétouan stands a few miles inland on the southern side of the Strait of Gibraltar, about sixty kilometers from Tangier. Five hundred years ago, a Muslim woman ruled over Tétouan. Spanish contemporaries referred to her as the Pirate Queen. Here, we shall call her Hurra of Tétouan, or simply Hurra, short for her nickname in Muslim sources, Sayyida al-hurra, which means the Free or Noble Woman.

Hurra witnessed the end of Muslim rule over the Iberian Peninsula, or as Muslims knew it, al-Andalus. At the turn of the sixteenth century, Spanish and Portuguese rulers had set out to conquer Muslim territories in al-Andalus and across the Straits of

Gibraltar in northwest Africa, or al-Maghrib. As a renewed form of the Crusades, the campaigns were launched as *Reconquista*: a taking back of Iberia from Muslims, whom they often called the Moors. Having lost her home to such attacks in childhood, Hurra fought against further encroachments on her ancestral homeland for almost half a century.

Scant details have reached us on Hurra. Even her name and identity remain shrouded in mystery. Some say her birth name was Aisha, but this remains uncertain.[2] Spanish contemporaries denigrated her by calling her a pirate, while most Muslim chroniclers ignored her altogether. Spanish sources acknowledged that she bore the title of Sultana, or female sovereign. The few Muslim sources that mention Hurra use the title Sitt al-Hurra – the Noble Lady.

Hurra of Tétouan was born around 1492, a fateful year that marks a turning point in world history. Most famously, in that year the Genoese-born navigator Christopher Columbus completed his first transatlantic voyage. The so-called discovery of the New World heralded transformations in economy, politics and culture on a global scale. That same year, the royal couple who had funded Columbus' naval mission expelled tens of thousands of Muslims and Jews from al-Andalus. Driving out non-Christians from al-Andalus and dispatching Columbus were two related steps in the *Reconquista*. Ferdinand of Aragon and Isabella of Castile, who had united their respective kingdoms with their marriage, saw no place for heathens in their expanding Catholic realm. Columbus had convinced the ruling couple they would reap great transatlantic riches. Christening his flagship as *La Santa María de la Immaculada Concepción* (The Holy Mary of the Immaculate Conception), reflects the religious aim of that undertaking as well. In retrospect, besides providing ample reserves of gold and silver, the New World came to be regarded as a new frontier for converting the local population to Christianity.

In the midst of all this, Hurra of Tétouan was a child. Her birthplace, Chefchaouen, was a town that her father had founded. She is said to have been named Hurra, or Aisha al-Hurra, after the mother of her father's friend and ally Abu Abdallah (Boabdil) Muhammad, the last Muslim ruler of Granada. Chefchaouen stands in present-day Morocco as a popular tourist destination, best known for its beautiful blue-painted walls and cobblestones.

Hurra's father Mulay Ali and his ancestors had strong ties to the region, reaching back to the eighth century when the early wave of Muslim warriors had arrived there. He had established himself in Chefchaouen in 1471, using it as a base in the Rif Mountains to attack Portuguese interests in Ceuta and Tangier, about 100 kilometers to the northeast and northwest respectively. Hurra's mother, Lalla Zohra Fernandez, came from the hilltops of Vejer de la Frontera, near the Spanish side of the Straits of Gibraltar.

By 1492, the Muslim presence had shaped Iberian history for over seven centuries. As early as 711, Arabs and their local allies controlled the maritime checkpoints between the Atlantic Ocean and the Mediterranean Sea. The principal passageway, Gibraltar, a distorted form of Jabal al-Tariq – "Tariq's Rock" – takes its name from Tariq, the commander of Muslim armies there.

Decades before Hurra's birth, the Portuguese prince Henry the Navigator, who often gets credit for initiating the Great Age of Discovery, had captured the strategic port of Ceuta in 1415. In 1437 his troops razed the port of Tétouan because they resented having a Muslim stronghold so close to their base in Ceuta. By 1471 their armies occupied Tangier and other Muslim strongholds, forcing thousands of people into slavery. Meanwhile, Spanish armies attacked Granada. By the time Columbus landed on the Caribbean coast, the last Muslim ruler of Granada had surrendered.

Growing up, Hurra received a good education from the most renowned members of the *ulama* in her native Chefchaouen. She could speak or understand Castilian and Portuguese as well as Arabic and probably at least one local Berber vernacular. Standing at the crossroads of both sea and land routes between the intellectual and trading center of Fez and the cities of al-Andalus, the small town claimed a rich traditional heritage. At the time, the quest for knowledge of Islamic learning and the *baraka* or spiritual potency of Sufi holy men and women were both markers of social distinction. And so was direct descent from the Prophet Muhammad. Hurra's clan claimed to be *sharif*s, or descendants of the Prophet. Her ancestor Ibn Mashish, who lived in the twelfth century, was a revered Sufi and a *sharif*. The nobility of her family was thus long established in the eyes of her contemporaries.

In 1510, Hurra married Muhammad al-Mandari, a young man from an important political family, originally from Granada. He had been governing Tétouan since 1505. Before long they had a daughter. Her husband's family had lost their estates in Granada to the *Reconquista*. Like his clansmen, Hurra's husband took pride in resisting foreign assaults on their homeland. His uncle Sidi Abu-al-Hasan was highly regarded for seizing Tétouan from the Portuguese and then for rebuilding the port and ensuring that Muslim commerce thrived. At its peak, Tétouan had trade connections that extended as far east as the Levant and as far north as Scandinavia.

Hurra's marriage to Muhammad strengthened the bond between two prominent clans. They joined forces in resisting Portuguese advances from the coast into inland mountainous regions. Her family connections and personal qualities made her an effective and valued partner. Her father ruled in Chefchaouen. Her brother had a high position at the court of the Sultan of Fez. Muhammad often sought her advice and trusted her with important matters in his absence from Tétouan. As the Moroccan scholar Hasna Lebbady observes, "She was trusted by her male relatives, and this seemed to be a feature of Andalusian-Moroccan women in general . . . She knew what needed to be done under different circumstances and these are the kinds of qualities that would have made her a leader."[3] This arrangement continued until her husband died – the exact date remains unknown, ranging from 1515 to 1529. Hurra then ruled independently, with her authority unquestioned for over a decade, maybe even two decades or more.

Portuguese and Spanish sources sought to stigmatize Hurra by labeling her as a pirate. Of course, the line separating renegade pirates and legitimate navigators depends on one's perspective. One side's corsair may be another side's admiral. To describe Hurra as a pirate, or a pirate-queen no less, would be to misrepresent her. In her time Tétouan was the only major Moroccan port that operated outside Portuguese control. The city itself did not have a fleet, so Hurra and her associates on both sides of the Straits of Gibraltar did indeed become partners with local privateers to attack Portuguese and Spanish ships. Lebbady observes that "Piracy was rampant in the 16th century and by no means limited to the southern coast of the Mediterranean . . . English pirates used to intercept the Spanish galleys coming back from the Americas, and what they took as booty was a major source of income for the government of Queen Elizabeth I."[4] European sources complain further that Hurra treated the ruler of Ceuta with utter contempt. They also report Muslims capturing and ransoming Christians. The fact is that Muslims and Christians both profited from this abhorrent practice. Such is war. Such is business.

For years, Hurra fought against the Portuguese king João III (r. 1521–1557), a grandson of Ferdinand and Isabella. Negotiations and short-lived truces punctuated episodes of confrontation between the two sides. Clashes had undeniable religious overtones, with each adversary considering the other the enemy of God. The *Reconquista* fed on Catholic fervor and, similarly, Hurra made clear gestures to emphasize her role as a defender of Islam. Drawing on common religious grounds, Hurra also reached out to the contemporary Ottoman Sultan Suleyman the Magnificent (r. 1520–1566).

The Ottoman Empire kept expanding with enormous momentum. In 1453, Ottoman Sultan Mehmet II had conquered Constantinople and renamed it Istanbul or Islambol (literally full of Islam, or the abode of Islam). With that victory he realized a long-standing wish. Half a century later, the Ottomans seemed unstoppable. From 1517 they had acquired a strong footing in Egypt and had taken many cities along the African coast of what are now Libya and Algeria. A formidable Ottoman ally ruled most of North Africa from his seat in Algiers, with the rank of Kapudan Pasha, or admiral, in the powerful Ottoman navy. European sources knew him (or maybe his brother; sources are ambiguous) as Barbarossa and vilified him as a pirate, as they did Hurra.

The Ottomans presented themselves as the champions of Islam. As such, they supported the enemies of their enemies. And the Portuguese were enemies. With Ottoman backing, mainly led by Barbarossa and his large fleet, Hurra pushed back the Portuguese and maintained control over Tétouan, not only after her husband's death but also after the death of her influential brother in 1539. However, the Ottomans soon realized that military and commercial collaboration did not have the returns they hoped and decided that Hurra was no longer needed. And when the Portuguese governor of Ceuta cut off commercial ties with Tétouan, local merchants grumbled. This was a serious situation and it required a strong response.

To strengthen her position, Hurra offered her hand in marriage to the powerful ruler of Fez, whom her brother had served. Their wedding in 1541 was a spectacle worthy of royalty. At the time, she was almost fifty and he was ten or so years her junior (his exact age is not known).

She did not go to him, he came to her. The Sultan transported himself, along with a group of companions, from Fez to Tétouan. Though a marriage of mutual political convenience, it was not conventional: from the outset husband and wife had agreed to live separately. Shortly after the ceremony the groom returned to Fez, leaving his bride in charge of her city. Hurra had hoped to rely on the political connections of her new husband to integrate the affairs of her realm with those of mainland Morocco. The Sultan treated her with great consideration, especially given that his own grip on power seemed uncertain. A new local clan was advancing on him from the south, with strong popular support and superior military prowess.

Hurra's half-brother and her son-in-law, the man who had married her only daughter, allied themselves with this new dynasty, betraying her and her new husband. On October 22, 1542 they came to Tétouan, accompanied by a group of cavalry-men, dethroned Hurra and broke away from Fez. She was exiled to Chefchaouen, where she spent the last years of her life.

Today, an artist's vision of Hurra welcomes visitors to the Chefchaouen Museum. Lebbady counts her among the "Andalusi-Moroccan heroines who populate the nation's history and folklore."[5]

# 10

## Pari Khanum
### (1548–1578)

## A GOLDEN LINK IN THE SAFAVID CHAIN OF COMMAND

The wind trembles like a willow branch before her tenderness
Timidly offering flowers as tribute.

(Early Safavid poet laureate, ca. 1575)

The history of Islam entered a new phase in the early modern period, the general title for the sixteenth and seventeenth centuries. At some points during this time, the Ottoman, Mughal, and Safavid dynasties ruled over vast territories extending as far west as the Balkans in Europe and as far east as the Malay Peninsula.

In Iran, formidable women stood behind the Safavid throne, but none as resolute, redoubtable and effective as Pari Khanum (1548–1578). Half a century before she was born, her grandfather, Shah Ismail I (r. 1501–1524), had founded the new dynasty, naming it after his clan's thirteenth-century ancestor Safi-al-Din Ardabili. A couple of decades after Pari Khanum had died, her nephew Shah Abbas I (r. 1588–1629) raised the dynasty to its highest point. He made the new Safavid capital, Isfahan, so magnificent that visitors said seeing it was equal to seeing half the entire world.

At the peak of their power, Safavid kings ruled over Iran from the Caspian Sea to the Persian Gulf north to south, and vast territories beyond, in what are now Afghanistan, Turkmenistan, Armenia, Georgia, Azerbaijan, Dagestan, Turkey and Iraq, from east to west.

As the dynasty's longest-reigning monarch, Shah Tahmasp (r. 1524–1576), Pari Khanum's father, brought stability to his expansive kingdom, establishing solid relations with multiple groups with conflicting interests. Silk-making flourished in his royal workshops, and the ancient city of Qazvin, which he chose as his capital in 1546, attracted men of letters, calligraphers and craftsmen, welcoming them all with its mild climate and beautiful Persian gardens. After centuries of living on the margins of societies not friendly to Shias, the Shia *ulama* gained a strong footing in Iran, for the Safavid kings keenly supported Shia scholars and scholarship. By the middle of the sixteenth century, hundreds of scholarly works had appeared under Safavid patronage. Then Sunni–Shia clashes that had remained dormant for generations re-erupted. The Safavids fanned the flames of sectarian conflict as a strategy to counter political, economic and ideological threats from the neighboring Ottoman Empire. The Ottomans reciprocated. However, in 1576, soon after the renewal of conflict, Tahmasp died, leaving behind a court torn by internal conflicts.

Pari Khanum was born in 1548, her father's twenty-fifth year on the Safavid throne. Court chroniclers report her date of birth as sometime between August 6 and September 4, a four-week window that in astrological terms augurs a strong Leo with a shade of Virgo (they took astrology seriously back then). Most chronicles record her name as Pari-Khan Khanum, which literally translates into something like the oxymoronic Lady-Sir Pari. Most likely this was not her given name at birth but a court title. The Persian word *pari*, a cognate for the English word *fairy*, makes a good name for a girl, so this may have been her birth name. Of course, it was uncommon, and considered disrespectful, to refer to royal women by their first names, so it would be natural to add Khanum, Turkish for "lady." Adding Khan, the Turkic word for "lord," to a woman's name might seem strange, but there was precedent, and Shah Tahmasp's own sister went by the same title, Pari-Khan Khanum. For the sake of clarity, we shall refer to the aunt as Pari Khanum I. Perhaps this odd combination of the male title Khan with the female Khanum deliberately conveys the notion of a woman who wields the authority most commonly reserved by men, for men.

Pari Khanum's place of birth lay a day's ride on horseback from Tabriz, the city that served as her father's capital at the time. Her mother was a princess-bride hailing from a powerful family in Circassia, the region along the eastern shore of the Black Sea in the Caucasus Mountains. Shah Ismail had sent his expectant wife into the freshness of the mountains near Tabriz, hoping that she and her baby would imbibe the spiritual potency or baraka that he thought the blessed trees and enchanted streams of the land embodied.

Shah Tahmasp showered the best of everything upon Pari Khanum, his favorite among seven daughters and twelve sons. He had multiple wives and multiple children. Appreciating Pari Khanum's wit and sweet manners, he wanted her to have the best possible education. Sources tell us that she learned horsemanship, archery, poetry and calligraphy, as well as Islamic law and jurisprudence. So she could read, write, think analytically, and ride as well.

When Pari Khanum was nine or ten the king betrothed his beloved daughter to the nephew he loved most. The young prince governed the remote province of Sistan, in southeast Iran, neighbouring present-day Pakistan, on the king's behalf. However, the marriage was never consummated, some say because Shah Tahmasp chose not to send Pari Khanum so far away from his side. However, that did not keep him from instigating the marriage, partly for the political significance of displaying full support for his nephew. Political marriages shaped the backdrop of women's roles in Safavid Persia. Princes and princesses married into other ruling clans and extended networks of loyalty, enhancing connections and also reaping additional dividends. Shah Ismail's mother, Marta, came from the royal house of the Christian kings of Trebizond. So did his grandmother, Teodora, also known as Despina Khatun. Through marriage, the Christian kings of Trebizond and the Shia-Muslim chieftains of pastoral nomads in northwest Iran forged an alliance against their common enemy the Ottomans. When the time came, Shah Ismail married the daughter of a Kurdish chieftain from Mosul. The daughter they had together, Pari Khanum I, played a decisive role in safeguarding Safavid sovereignty through her serial political marriages. Following a crushing defeat by Ottoman cannon fire in the Battle of Chaldiran (1514), Safavid survival partly depended on having alliances with princely families around the western and southern basins of the Caspian Sea. In pursuit of this policy Pari Khanum I first married the king of Shirvan, then the king of Gilan, and then the ruler of Shaki (in Azerbaijan). She later settled with her own first cousin, a state dignitary from the Istajlu clan within the Qizilbash confederacy that formed the backbone of the Safavid military might.

At the turn of the sixteenth century, the Qizilbash confederacy of warriors had sworn allegiance to Shah Ismail. They crowned him when he was merely thirteen years old. Organized more like a Sufi order than an ethnic or tribal alliance, the Qizilbash confederacy united the devotees of the Sufi master Safi-al-Din Ardabili, who lived in the thirteenth to fourteenth centuries, and from whom Safavid kings were descended. Shah Ismail built his far-reaching kingdom in reliance on Qizilbash military prowess. The clans that formed the core of the Qizilbash confederacy remained powerful under Shah Tahmasp, often competing to influence critical decisions within and outside the Safavid court.

Scholars commonly emphasize three foundations for Safavid power: Qizilbash might, Persian political know-how, and a potent brew of Shia-Islamic ideology. However, any account of early

Safavid success remains partial and inaccurate without acknowledging a fourth foundation: the elite women of the court.

To portray Safavid women as mere tokens of political exchange
or trophy objects is to fall short of historical reality. Pari Khanum
is a case in point. She did not rise to the height of political power
because of marriage. In fact, unlike most other women of the
Safavid court, and indeed most women of her time, she never
went to her groom's house. Of course, being the king's daughter
helped, but Shah Tahmasp had other daughters too, none of
whom matched her.

Pari Khanum was in her early twenties when Shah Tahmasp
began to seek her advice on all matters, from the trivial to the
most substantive. Knowing the court's secrets and having access
to its resources, she gave her confident opinion on politics,
commerce and finance. She had to vie with Prince Heydar (1556–
1576), her younger brother from another mother, who also
enjoyed their father's love and trust. Encouraging his son's political skills, Shah Tahmasp even occasionally deputed him to
preside over regular court sessions.

Rivalries escalated when the king became ill and almost died
in the fall of 1574. Uncertainties simmered. Who was going to
succeed Shah Tahmasp? What position would the Qizilbash
warriors, Persian administrators and Shia *ulama* be taking? Pari
Khanum made it a priority to nurse her father back to health.
Shah Tahmasp recovered and continued to reign from his bed
for another year and a half. He eventually died at night on May
14, 1576. His death left many questions unresolved.

Clashes broke out immediately. As a woman, Pari Khanum
had no viable chance of succeeding to the Safavid throne. There
was no precedent in that dynasty. Her half-brother, Prince
Heydar, had two older brothers ahead of him in line. The first,
Prince Mohammad, had nothing to recommend him. Poor
eyesight and a poorer moral reputation disqualified him. The
next son, Ismail, who was named after the founder of the dynasty,

had given his father so much grief that Shah Tahmasp had banished him from 1557. Meanwhile, leaders of the Qizilbash had their ranks split, the Persian bureaucrats remained neutral, and the *ulama* stayed aloof but conspired in the background. This complicated situation left enough room for Heydar to maneuver his way upward and for Pari Khanum to stay steadfast.

Being the only adult son at his father's deathbed, Heydar made his move. Counting on the support of his mother and kinsmen, as well as factions of the Qizilbash, he crowned himself as Heydar Shah. His mother provided a will or decree, seemingly in the late king's hand, that named her own son as his heir-apparent. Others had doubts. In the words of a chronicler, "With the arrogance of youth, and natural ambition, [Heydar] considered himself the heir-apparent."[1]

Even before Shah Tahmasp's death Heydar had conspired to eliminate his half-brother Ismail. Pari Khanum had caught wind of this and thwarted the plan. Stirring fatherly affections in the dying king, she reminded him of Ismail's bravery and reminisced about the night that the stern king had surprised everyone by dancing at his son's wedding. Her words shook him enough that he despatched a party of Qizilbash musketeers with orders to guard the fortress where his son was kept under watch.

Sensing a potential threat from Pari Khanum, Heydar confined her mobility and restricted her access to people and resources. Fearful of what might come next, she threw herself at her brother's mercy and pleaded with his mother, assuring them both that she was wholeheartedly committed to honoring and obeying him as king. For one thing, she promised to win over the loyalty of her Circassian kinsmen, especially her powerful uncle, the formidable Shamkhal Khan.

Meanwhile, part of the Qizilbash leadership rejected Heydar's claim. Unlike the Istajlus who backed Heydar's succession, other powerful warrior Qizilbash factions declared in favor of Ismail. Ismail was their fellow warrior, unlike Heydar who spent his time conspiring with the women of the harem. Strategically, Ismail's succession could bring more stability. Qizilbash warriors released Ismail and pledged allegiance to him, hoping to place him on the throne. The success of their plan hinged on Pari Khanum supporting it from within the royal complex in Qazvin. She rose to the challenge.

First, she questioned the authenticity of the document that Heydar and his mother had brought to light. Suggesting that Shah Tahmasp's handwriting had been forged in the harem, Pari Khanum implicated Heydar's mother. As two princess-brides, the thirty-something Georgian mother of Heydar and the forty-something Circassian mother of Pari Khanum had a long rivalry. It may be that in sympathy with her own mother, Pari Khanum harbored a preference for her other half-brother. Shamkhal Khan, her mother's redoubtable brother, agreed.

Getting the keys to the entrance gates from Pari Khanum, Shamkhal Khan and Ismail's Qizilbash allies stormed the royal complex and seized Heydar. Within hours, soldiers had torn him apart, limb from limb, and hurled the parts down from the parapets, much to the horror of those who had come to rescue the prince. Wanting to add insult to injury, Safavid chroniclers say that the 22-year-old prince had put on a disguise and hidden in the women's quarters, failing to act like a man. They blame the atrocities on Pari Khanum. Even a modern historian insists, uncritically, that Pari Khanum had "resorted to a ruse in order to win the day," duping Heydar by taking and then breaking her pledge to him. To blame her for the way her half-brother died seems going too far.

Whether Pari Khanum wanted it or not, a new chapter had opened in her life. With the royal complex under attack, she sealed the treasury to safeguard what she could from looting. She saved the women of the harem, including Heydar's mother as well as the wives, sisters and daughters of the murdered prince's allies within the court. On her orders, all princes and top-ranking leaders of the Qizilbash assembled at Qazvin's congregational mosque on Friday May 23, 1576. Less than ten days after Shah Tahmasp died, she pledged allegiance to Ismail II as king, *in absentia.*

Waiting for the new king to arrive, Pari Khanum oversaw the affairs of the court and the state. Minor unrest stirred in Qazvin, but she ruled firmly. During this interregnum, the notables took their orders from her. After their morning prayers every day, Qizilbash leaders proceeded to her residence for an audience, bringing "to her notice pressing administrative and financial problems. None dared to contravene her order."[2] This arrangement lasted for several weeks, even after Ismail's arrival.

Qizilbash chieftains, high-ranking officials and other notables continued their daily audience with Pari Khanum, first reporting to her and then to the new king. In the words of a Safavid chronicler who wrote a generation after these events, Pari Khanum's stewards, attendants and ladies-in-waiting "began to act with greater pomp and circumstance than during the reign of Shah Tahmasp, and her doorkeepers, chamberlains, and other retainers instituted ceremonies more appropriate to the court of a king." The tinge of prejudice in his tone is hard to miss.

Before long, however, Pari Khanum fell from grace. First, the new king forbad Qizilbash leaders and high-ranking officials to set foot in her palace. He often repeated this line to them, "Have you not understood, my friends, that interference in matters of state by women is demeaning to the king's honor?"[3] Knowingly or not, Islamil II was parroting what he had heard from the *ulama.* The statement that Abu Bakra had attributed to the Prophet after the Battle of the Camel, criticizing Aisha, appeared in Shia sources as well. Should Ismail II grant Pari Khanum an audience himself, he made sure to clarify in no uncertain terms that he sat on the throne, not her. He now wielded the power she had been instrumental in handing to him.

Long years in prison had hardened Ismail, inside and out. He was impatient, impulsive, cynical and insecure. Violently wary of the people around him, he made every day of his reign brim with vengeance and blood. He broke the promise he had made to his brothers upon arrival, to love them "like no other king ever treated his brothers."[4] Left and right, he slaughtered Safavid princes, his own brothers, cousins and nephews. In one day alone he had six of them murdered. On another occasion he had several hundred Sufis massacred. He sidelined the Qizilbash chieftains and alienated the Shia *ulama*, going against the policies set in place by his father and grandfather. Ismail's eighteen-month-long reign of terror came to an end with his death on November 25, 1577, probably of an overdose of opium, perhaps in combination with wine.[5]

Later Safavid chroniclers did not miss the opportunity to insinuate that Pari Khanum had a hand in getting rid of him, though there was no proof of this whatsoever. For example:

> The physicians discovered traces of poison in the Shah's body. Various conjectures emerged about his murder: One had it that the Shah had spurned Pari Khanom again, and she had conspired with maidservants of the harem to put poison in his medication.[6]

Ismail II stopped short of killing his sister and Pari Khanum survived his reign of terror. To prevent unrest upon the king's death, Pari Khanum shuttered the gates of the palace complex and took charge of affairs. She had the backing of the women of the harem and the administrative elite at the court. Qizilbash chieftains had reservations about this, and the *ulama* objected to having a woman on the throne. But options were limited. They could go with Ismail II's eight-month-old son or with Tahmasp's eldest son, Prince Mohammad. In spite of eliminating all potential contenders to the throne, the dead ruler had spared his full brother, perhaps taking pity on the man's poor health and failing eyesight, and noticing that the weakling had a bad reputation as an opium addict, a drunk, and a debauchee. His time had arrived. In effect, Pari Khanum took control of the court as a regent for the second time in less than two years. As one of her most urgent steps in restoring peace and stability, she freed all the notables that Ismail II had imprisoned.

Prince Mohammad and his ambitious wife refused to keep Pari Khanum in power. On their way to Qazvin they launched a smear campaign against her, circulating rumors that she and her rebellious Circassian uncle had conspired to overthrow Safavid rule and to undermine Shia Islam. Still, when the nominated king's entourage arrived outside the capital on February 12, 1578, Pari Khanum went out to welcome them with great pomp and ceremony. Sitting in a gold-woven domed litter, she had brought hundreds of women, men and eunuchs with her. Seeing the extent of the influence and authority that Pari Khanum exercised, Prince Mohammad's wife kissed her sister-in-law's hand, but not without malice.

The very first day that Mohammad ascended the Safavid throne, he sent guards to seize control of the treasury from Pari Khanum and ordered her death, along with any other contenders for the throne including Ismail II's toddler. Men intercepted Pari Khanum on the road, on her way back to her palace from the new king's inauguration festivities, riding in the same gold-woven dome from which she had welcomed him and his wife a few days earlier. She was scarcely twenty-nine when they strangled her and broke her neck.

Pari Khanum's short but intrepid life highlights the decisive role that royal women played in sixteenth-century Shia-Muslim Iran. Her ingenious and effective interventions rescued the Safavids at moments when their power base almost imploded. Safavid sources acknowledge her as the most powerful Safavid woman. While contemporary chroniclers and panegyrists praised her sharp insight and practical competence, later historians judged her harshly, denigrating her as a malicious, self-serving and conniving woman who plotted the murder of two of her brothers. No doubt misrepresenting and distorting her biography served those in power at the time, but these biases have also been echoed with approval in modern scholarship. Trusting the chronicles too much, a twentieth-century Orientalist uncritically cited "the irresponsible character of the 'shadow government' represented by the harem, the Queen Mother and the eunuchs,"[7] among "the more conspicuous factors" that led to the decline of the Safavid state. Contemporary encyclopedias repeat the typically misogynistic accusations of sixteenth- and seventeenth-century chroniclers, particularly blaming Pari Khanum's ruse to win the day. Writing in the second edition of the *Encyclopaedia of Islam*, which stands as a major reference work, an acknowledged authority on Safavid history avers, "With the *connivance* of Isma'il's sister [emphasis added], Pari Khan Khanum, the conspirators placed poison in an electuary containing opium, which was consumed by Isma'il and one of his boon-companions."[8]

Rather than taking sides in history by either condemning or exonerating Pari Khanum, it would be better to examine and appraise her conduct in the light of the volatile climate in which she lived, measuring her decisions against the background of the shifting balance of power amongst the Qizilbash, the *ulama*, the administrators and other rival factions. Right or wrong, she was an agent of historical decision-making and action.

# 11

# Nur Jahan
## (1577–1645)

## LIGHT OF THE WORLD

A t the end of October 1577 a comet appeared in the night sky. Known as the Great Comet, this astronomical phenomenon stirred strong mixed feelings across the globe. In India its blood-red light and fiery course conjured up fears of impending upheaval. People believed it augured calamity such as war, fire, pestilence and a change of dynasty. Nur Jahan was born a few months earlier, in February, that same year. Writing a couple of generations later, Mughal chroniclers took the comet as heralding her extraordinarily eventful life.

Nur Jahan (1577–1645) was unbreakable. As an infant, her parents abandoned her to die by a roadside outside the city of Kandahar, now in Afghanistan. She survived. Decades later, the ruling emperor, Jahangir (r. 1605–1627), executed her beloved elder brother. In the same year, 1607, the emperor also had her husband hacked into pieces. After a lucky second marriage and almost twenty years of good fortune, the tide turned against her again. Jahangir's successor had her son-in-law murdered, fearing possible competition from him. Despite all the odds, Nur Jahan walked through life with dignified resolve.

During her brightest years, 1608–1627, Nur Jahan ruled over the Mughal Empire – one of the most glorious empires in human history. At its peak, it included much of what is now India, Pakistan, Afghanistan and Bangladesh. Nur Jahan, "Light of the World," is her imperial title, which overshadows her given name at birth.

India's Mughal dynasty (1526–1857) traced its lineage to the Mongolian warlord Timur (ca. 1336–1405), better known in English as Tamerlane. Timur's great-grandson inherited his world-conquering ambitions more than a century later (ca. 1483–1530), taking on the *nom de guerre* of Babur, which means "tiger." With a combination of military might and diplomatic skill, Babur marched into India and soon prevailed. He made pacts with those local Hindu and Muslim rulers who accepted his suzerainty; he uprooted those who did not. Within decades, Babur's most capable descendent, the Emperor Akbar, tripled the size of his realm, expanding Mughal power across the Indian subcontinent. Akbar's long reign, 1556–1605, stands out as an era of growth, prosperity and cultural flowering in the long and rich history of India.

Nur Jahan entered the Mughal realm as an outsider, the infant daughter of a migrant. She was a few months old when her parents brought her to India in 1578. Nobody could foresee at the time that decades later she would reign alongside the ruling emperor's son, with the title of Nur Jahan, "Light of the World." The future queen's father had fled from the Safavid-ruled city of Herat, where chaos ruled after Shah Tahmasp's death in 1576. On her father's side, Nur Jahan's clan belonged to a faction that had supported the losing candidate in the bloody wars of succession to the Safavid throne in Iran. India seemed like an obvious destination, partly because the Mughal and Safavid courts shared a common language, Persian. Before Nur Jahan's father, hundreds, not to say thousands, of Persian-speaking administrators, secretaries, accountants, scribes, poets and others had found patronage in and outside the fabulously rich courts of the Mughals and their regional allies.

However, the journey to the heart of India was proverbially arduous. In a moment of despair, baby Nur Jahan had been abandoned on the roadside, only to be rescued and reunited with her parents within hours. Finally, the family made it to Akbar's court, held in the reddish fortress of Fatehpur Sikri in northern India. Within months of their arrival, family connections helped her father get an audience with the emperor and find employment there. Well-schooled in courtly etiquette and administrative know-how, the man quickly rose in the courtly ranks.

Akbar readily appointed capable men to high office, almost regardless of their ethnic, regional or religious background. Nur Jahan's parents were Shia Muslims, unlike Akbar who professed Sunni Islam. In the words of a contemporary chronicler, "Followers of various religions had a place in the broad scope of [this] peerless empire – unlike other countries of the world, like Iran, where there is room for only Shiites, and Rum, Turan, and Hindustan, where there is room only for Sunnis."[1]

Growing up in her father's *haveli*, a sprawling family home, Nur Jahan had two older brothers, an older sister, and two younger siblings. She took lessons at home in basic rhetoric, logic and arithmetic. She memorized passages from the Quran, some hadith, and scores of lines of verse, mostly in Persian. By the age of fourteen, she had developed a taste for good food, fine poetry and exacting calligraphy. She also learned how to ride, shoot and hunt. When she reached seventeen, in 1594, her parents married her off to a suitable husband. He was a warrior, who had once fought and killed a tiger or lion barehanded. For that, they called him Sher-Afgan, "Lion-Slayer." He belonged to the same extended clan as his new wife and was a Shia Muslim. Like the bride's father and elder brothers, he, too, was a Mughal official, and like the rest of the family probably spoke Persian at home.

As the wife of a Mughal official, Nur Jahan accompanied her husband to the province of Bengal, 1,200 kilometers away from her parents. Shrines, temples and ashrams dotted the beautiful landscape, with Sufi's sadhus, yogis and other holy men passing through. Her husband had to spend long periods of time away from home, overseeing the collection of taxes and fighting off bandits. The birth of their only child, a girl, in 1600 or 1601, marked a high point in the couple's married life. They named her Ladli, an affectionate word meaning "beloved" in the Bengali language. As a wife and mother, Nur Jahan kept active. She had a keen eye for detail and a sharp analytical mind. The couple's stay in Bengal ended soon after Akbar died in 1605.

For the most part, Akbar's 36-year-old son, who succeeded him to the Mughal throne in 1605, continued his policies. He took on the title of Jahangir – "Conqueror of the World". Nur Jahan's family continued to thrive under the new ruler's patronage.

Her father and brothers had influence at the imperial court. Jahangir knew the family well and had betrothed one of Nur Jahan's nieces to his eldest son. Some say that he himself may have had an interest in her, but this may well have been a contemporary rumor or a fabrication of later chroniclers. Yet relations between Nur Jahan's politically influential family and the new emperor became fragile. A couple of years after Jahangir's accession to the Mughal throne, a conspiracy against him came to light, and in the summer or fall of 1607 he had Nur Jahan's older brother Mohammad executed on suspicion of complicity. Her father was demoted in rank, forced to pay a penalty and spent some time in prison. Similarly accused, Nur Jahan's husband, too, was killed within a few months.

Taking the forfeited property of defeated enemies into the emperor's treasury and taking their wives, daughters, sisters and sometimes mothers into the harem was a matter of routine. Thus, Nur Jahan found herself and Ladli in the imperial harem. This was at once a gesture of reconciliation towards her family and a warning: the welfare of their daughter and granddaughter now depended on their continued loyalty to Jahangir.

Women of the imperial household spent most of their time sequestered in the harem. Although co-wives often plotted against one another, vying for attention from their shared husband, they sometimes formed bonds of camaraderie. Almost instantly Nur Jahan came to the attention of powerful elders. She was thirty-four, widowed and had a daughter from her marriage. Impressed by her intelligence and competence, women of the harem took her under their wing, taking their cue from none other than Jahangir's own mother. Frequently, senior women of the harem provided counsel to the ruler and his courtiers. When the chance presented itself, they vouched for Nur Jahan in Jahangir's presence, and the empror took her hand. Ironically, the turning point in Nur Jahan's life resulted from a combination of unlikely events that brought her under the direct gaze of the killer of her brother and her husband. As a later chronicler put it,

> The days of misfortune drew to a close, and the stars of her good fortune commenced to shine, and to wake as from a deep sleep ... [On] a certain New Year's festival, she attracted the love and the affection of the king. She was soon made the favorite wife of his majesty.[2]

The wedding took place on May 11, 1611. By one count, the king had taken nineteen wives before that because his alliance-building initiatives hinged on political marriage. His nuptial ties reflected the political connections that he fostered. Most of the women in Jahangir's harem, his wives and others, were there as part of political negotiations. In this, he followed the example set by his imperial ancestors, especially Babur and Akbar. His women came from the families of Muslim potentates, Rajput chieftains, Kashmiri Sufis, Tibetan rajas and others. After Jahangir too, the Mughal harem continued to embody the unity of the diversely scattered ruling elite of the realm. Naturally, taking Nur Jahan's hand in marriage brought benefits for her family. Her father received a promotion in rank and a substantial increase in his imperial stipend. The road opened for the advancement of her surviving older brother.

Soon, Nur Jahan became Jahangir's queen and co-sovereign. Her advance was groundbreaking. Within years, she wielded more power than any other woman in India, and maybe the world at that time. She embodied and projected authority like no other woman in Mughal history. Before her, Mughal women had established precedent in issuing official decrees, signing as "mother of," "daughter of," "sister of" or "wife of" the ruler. Nur Jahan broke new ground by signing decrees as sovereign. One biographer, Ruby Lal, observes, "that signature speaks volumes." Even though her name was not mentioned in congregational Friday prayers, she did wield the two other official signs of sovereignty: she issued edicts and had coins struck in her name. Within a few years after Nur Jahan's marriage to Jahangir, gold and silver coins bearing her name began to circulate. Some had Jahangir's name on the obverse and hers on the reverse; some coins only had hers. A half-ounce gold coin, measuring nearly an inch in diameter, which is now kept at a museum in Lucknow, Pakistan, reads:

> By the order of King Jahangir,
> Gold gained a hundred glories
> Bearing the name of Queen Nur-Jahan.[3]

Members of the court and people on the street alike noticed the tokens and the palpable effects of Nur Jahan's ascendancy. She exercised a direct and visible kind of power. In effect, she ruled jointly with her husband. Some, like Thomas Roe (1581–1644), who served as Britain's envoy in India during the 1620s, viewed her as the true power in the realm. Writing disdainfully about the relations between Jahangir and Nur Jahan, Roe observes, "[She] governs him, and wynds him up at her pleasure."[4]

How did she amass so much power and influence? First, by her wit and charm. Even more important was her gritty loyalty and protective devotion toward Jahangir. Last but not least was her family's prolonged record of high-level service to the Mughal court.

Two anecdotes illustrate her charisma. Setting out on elephant back, together with a full hunting retinue, on a spring day in 1617, she spotted stripes in the distance, fired six musket shots, and bagged four tigers in the wild. In sheer delight, Jahangir showered her with coins. In another episode, almost ten years later, when a rebellious warlord kidnapped Jahangir for ransom in 1626, Nur Jahan personally led the imperial troops to his rescue.

The many vicissitudes of her life had equipped Nur Jahan with an ability to be both kind and firm in the same breath. That rare combination enabled her to keep Jahangir on the throne far longer than he could have survived without her by his side.

Notwithstanding his imperial title of Jahangir, The World-conqueror, the fourth Mughal emperor was focused more on pleasure than the pursuit of power. Ruby Lal, Nur Jahan's biographer, characterizes him as "an aesthete." Jahangir kept a journal and recorded how everything and everyone he encountered stirred a sense of wonderment in him: a conversation with an ascetic, rubies and sapphires, seedless grapes. He traveled with a pair of domesticated lovebirds, which he named Layla and Majnun after a pair of famous lovers in folk literature. Every day he would go out to observe the birds and make detailed notes. He was curious about plants, poems, paintings and philosophical questions. He loved to learn.

Jahangir had a connoisseur's eye for the arts. Nur Jahan was his match and they received architects, musicians, poets, and painters at the court. Among other forms of artistic work, they encouraged the replication and adaptation of European works brought by Jesuit missionaries.

The emperor's predilection for beauty and pleasure would not have mattered so much to the imperial household had he not been an addict. But he was. He had taken to drinking wine when he was eighteen. Soon, wine failed to soothe him, and so he turned to stronger spirits. He would take twenty cups of doubly distilled spirits, fourteen during the daytime and the rest at night. The habit of drink ran in the family, and two of Jahangir's brothers died of alcoholism. Although Islamic law forbids it, the use and abuse of intoxicants abounded among the Mughals, from the court to the street. Jahangir's hand shook so much that he could not drink from his own cup. Later, to induce the thrill he no longer experienced from alcohol, he added opium and other sedatives to his daily regimen.

Nur Jahan made a decisive intervention. Finding her husband emotionally fragile and dependent on intoxicants grieved her. She resolved to stop his suffering from shaking limbs, chronic respiratory troubles and other ailments that addiction had caused or worsened. As Jahangir recorded in his personal journal, the queen "lessened my wine by degrees, and kept me from things that did not suit me."[5] Keeping a powerful man from things that may not suit him is a hazardous undertaking that few have the courage to enact. Fights may have erupted, but both parties knew the stakes were high. Her effective intervention helped prolong Jahangir's hold on power for at least a decade longer than it would have lasted otherwise.

And Jahangir loved Nur Jahan for that and more. She had his faith, trust and love. He relied on her. The king's journal reflects a general lack of interest in writing about any wives except her. The self-absorbed and megalomaniac king hailed his favorite wife as "the one most fond of him." Walking in the garden on a sunny day, he placed himself before her in such a way that the shadow of his body reached the queen's feet. With one step, he humbled himself for his queen while keeping up appearances for those with him. In his own inimitable imperial way, he threw himself at her feet. Mughal sources are normally taciturn, but these episodes give a sense of of the real flesh and blood royals.

When Jahangir died in 1627, Nur Jahan's fall from grace came all too suddenly. His third son and successor, Shah Jahan, who had been born to a Rajput woman, eyed his mother's co-wife with resentment. He feared that the formidable Nur Jahan would mobilize the court against him and in favor of a rival Mughal prince. Within a few weeks of taking power, the arrogant 35-year-old emperor killed his half-brother from a different mother. The boy he killed had married Ladli and so was Nur Jahan's son-in-law. Shah Jahan had himself married Nur Jahan's niece, Mihrunissa. Still, his love for his wife did not lessen his animosity toward her aunt. Obviously afraid of his father's once all-powerful consort, Shah Jahan dashed any hopes that the queen may have had for reconciliation. He sent her into exile, along with her now-widowed daughter.

When Shah Jahan's beloved young wife, Mihrunissa, died in 1631, he built a worthy tribute to her: the mausoleum called the Taj Mahal. This magnificent structure stands as one of the wonders of the world to this day. Ironically, the Taj Mahal reflects the vision of Nur Jahan. A decade earlier, she had designed a memorial garden in honor of her parents. Inside the spectacular garden stood a rectangular building made entirely of white marble inlaid with semi-precious gems, colored mosaic tiles and stone latticework. This was the earthly paradise on the banks of the Yamuna River where she had the bodies of her parents interred, in ochre cenotaphs under an ornamental vault. Years later, the Taj Mahal was built right across from it, on the other side of the river. On a larger scale, the same template was followed, down to the details of the red lilies and rose petals in the paintings and inlays. Nur Jahan's spirit haunts the greatest legacy of her tormenter.

# 12

# Safiye Sultan
## (ca. 1550–ca. 1619)

## A MOTHER OF MANY KINGS

When Sultan Murat III (r. 1574–1595) died in 1595, Safiye arranged for her 29-year-old son Mehmet to succeed his father on the Ottoman throne. That would make her the Sultan's mother, or Valide Sultan. Yes, here again, the identity and status of a woman is defined in terms of her relation to a man, as in the "daughter of so-and-so," "wife of so-and-so" or "sister of so-and-so." However, the Valide Sultan held one of the most powerful positions in the entire Ottoman Empire. Foreign envoys quickly learned that to get anything done there, they needed first and foremost to honor the Sultan's mother.

From the fourteenth century to the early twentieth century, forty-one Ottoman sultans ruled as Muslim sovereigns. At the turn of the seventeenth century, the Ottoman Empire stretched thousands of miles east to west and north to south: from Bosnia and Albania in the Balkans, across Greece and Turkey, to the Ethiopian coast in east Africa to Yemen in the south of the Arabian Peninsula; from Morocco to Egypt, and from Syria to Iraq and parts of Iran. Had the Ottoman sieges of Vienna succeeded in defeating the Habsburgs, some historians speculate that the course of human history might have been radically different. Ottoman influence even extended as far as South-East Asia, as an ally of the rulers of Aceh Darussalam. The history of Islam for well over half a millennium overlaps with that of the lands, seas and peoples that the Ottomans ruled.

All forty-one Ottoman rulers held the same title, Sultan, but some were more capable than others. The names of Sultan Mehmet the Conqueror (r. 1444–1446, 1451–1481), who conquered Constantinople in 1453, and Suleiman the Magnificent (r. 1520–1566), who ruled the longest, outshine the rest.

After Suleiman the Magnificent died in 1566, the Ottoman dynasty failed to produce illustrious sultans for over a century. Meanwhile, Valide Sultans held the dynasty and the empire together. For example, Safiye outshone her son, two grandsons and a great-grandson who succeeded one another to the throne during her lifetime. Noting that behind every incompetent, mentally defective or otherwise lackluster Sultan stood a sane and skillful woman, Ottoman historians refer to this period as the "Sultanate of women."

Safiye came from the mountainous Dukagjin highlands in northern Albania, near Kosovo. Some historians have assumed, incorrectly, that she came from a noble Venetian family. In fact, she was probably born into a Christian household around 1550 and given a different name at birth. When she was presented as a slave-girl, or concubine, to the young Ottoman Prince Murat (1546–1595), the future Sultan Murat III, he named her Safiye, which means "purely chosen."

The roots of slavery reached very deep in Ottoman history, and slaves performed myriad functions, from military service to mining to menial domestic work. Warlords and slave drivers seized boys, girls, men and women on the border zones of the empire, often around the Black Sea, the Caucasus Mountains or Sub-Saharan Africa, and sold them in urban slave markets. Much of this fell within the definition of *devsirme*, a form of tribute collection. From the fifteenth through the mid-seventeenth century, Balkan Christians were conscripted into the elite corps of the Janissaries, the Sultan's personal slave soldiers. Although Ottoman slavery differed from the later transatlantic slave trade in many ways, the very notion of treating human beings as objects is equally repugnant anywhere. Women and girls constituted the majority of slaves, often serving as *jariyas*, concubines. A very few of these ended up in the royal harem, as Safiye did.

In 1566, Safiye bore a son, the future heir to the Ottoman throne. Prince Murat adored her, so much so that it concerned his mother, who mistook her young son's lack of interest in other women as a sign of his being impotent. His dedication to Safiye did not diminish after he succeeded to the throne in 1573. Less than a year into his reign, Murat III declared Safiye to be his Haseki, or exclusive consort. Sultan Murat III's mother, the Venetian Valide Sultan Nurbanu (ca. 1525–1583), kept accusing Safiye of preventing Murat from taking opportunities to procreate more children with other women in the interests of the dynasty.[1] Nurbanu further accused Safiye's household personnel of withholding evidence and had them chained, tortured and sent into exile.[2] Eventually, Murat took other concubines, putting an end to the rumors by fathering at least twenty-three sons and twenty-eight daughters.

Sultan Murat III had Safiye by his side at the New Royal Palace, which is now called the Topkapi Palace in Istanbul. In that palace, the gifted royal architect Sinan (ca. 1490–1588) had designed and built a beautiful fountain chamber in 1579, where the Sultan spent hours in conversation with his favorite consort.

Safiye's standing improved further after Nurbanu died in 1583. As the most powerful woman of the harem, she could freely display her generosity. At the wedding procession for her daughter Fatma in 1593, Safiye had thousands of shiny new coins scattered around for onlookers to collect from the ground as the bride, concealed behind a red curtain, rode through the crowd to her husband's home.

Safiye's powers only increased when her husband died and her son became sultan. One of the early interventions she made as Valide Sultan, the new king's mother, was to suspend the sentence of drowning in the Bosphorus as a punishment for adulterous women. She took it upon herself to overrule the eunuch who served as Istanbul's mayor and practiced such a cruelty, saying that her son had appointed him to run the city, not to kill women. An eyewitness reported that:

> The Queene Mother, with the Grand Sultana and other of the Grand Signiors women, walking in their serraglio espyed a number of boates upon the river hurrying together. The Queene Mother sent to enquire of the matter; who was told that the Vizier did justice upon certaine chabies that is, whoores. Shee, taking displeasure, sent word and advised the eunuch Bassa that her sonne had left him to governe the citie and not to devoure the women; commanding him to looke well to the other businesse and not to meddle any more with the women till his masters returne.[3]

Safiye had a talent for diplomacy. A Venetian envoy once described her as "a woman of her word, trustworthy, and I can say that in her alone have I found truth in Constantinople."[4] Safiye's correspondence with Queen Elizabeth I of England (r. 1558–1603) shows her international standing.[5] In the first letter she wrote to Elizabeth, dated December 4, 1593, Safiye thanks the English sovereign for the gifts she had sent to her and Murat III, which were "full of marvels . . . [and more fragrant] than pure camphor and ambergris." Written in twenty-four lines on a single sheet of paper sprinkled with gold dust, the letter opens with "He is the Helper," in English on the top right hand of the page. Five colors of ink are used: black, blue, crimson, gold and scarlet. She begins with invoking the name of God and the blessings of Prophet Muhammad. She then introduces herself as mother of the heir to Murat, whose extensive domains she lists. Safiye greets the recipient as the crowned ruler of England, who follows Jesus and whom princes obey; a woman in the path of Mary, the chaste and virtuous.

As one member of royalty to another, Safiye promises to give Elizabeth friendship and support. The fact that Elizabeth had sent her, among other things, ten garments made from cloth of gold and a portrait of herself indicates that the English queen acknowledged the high royal standing of the recipient. In the language of diplomacy, gift exchange expressed a mutual acknowledgment of authority as well as friendship and alliance.

Most of all, Safiye cherished an ornate coach that the English Queen sent her. She had it properly covered and used it for excursions outside the palace complex, much to the dismay of those who preferred all women to be sequestered. One of the most widely circulated portraits of Queen Elizabeth shows her wearing a Turkish costume which may have been sent to her by Safiye. These exchanges between Safiye and Elizabeth highlight the diplomatic relationship between England and the Ottoman Empire. In a letter from 1599, Safiye responds to Elizabeth's request for good relations between the two realms:

> I have received your letter ... God-willing, I will take action in accordance with what you have written. Be of good heart in this respect. I constantly admonish my son, the Padishah, to act according to the treaty. I do not neglect to speak to him in this manner. God-willing, may you not suffer grief in this respect. May you too always be firm in friendship. God-willing, may [our friendship] never die. You have sent me a carriage and it has been delivered. I accept it with pleasure. And I have sent you a robe, a sash, two large gold-embroidered bath towels, three

handkerchiefs, and a ruby and pearl tiara. May you excuse [the unworthiness of the gifts].[6]

In retrospect, Safiye's patronage and funding of architectural monuments make up her longest-lasting accomplishment. The construction and maintenance of mosques, madrasas, hospitals, baths and the like reflected not only the wealth and influence but also the patron's piety and benevolence. Most famously, Safiye allocated funds for building a new Friday mosque, known as Yeni Cemii. Started in 1597, the mosque remained incomplete for over fifty years, only to be finished in 1665 by a later Valide Sultan, Turhan Hatice, mother of Mehmed IV.

For most of the time that she enjoyed the status of Valide Sultan, Safiye received a large stipend from the court, which amounted to the equivalent of three thousand silver coins (aspers) a day.[7] At some point in 1600 a rebellion broke out against her, when the imperial cavalry objected that, with Safiye's support, a mother and son had amassed over fifty million aspers. The woman, named Esperanza Malchi, served as Safiye's *kari*. The word *kari*, which means "woman" in Greek, was used in Ottoman Istanbul to refer to a non-Muslim (typically Jewish) woman who acted as a go-between for women of the harem and the outside world, serving as a confidante as well as business agent and secretary. Evidence suggests that Safiya's *kari* was quite an enterprising and ambitious woman herself. In a letter she wrote to Queen Elizabeth, also possibly dated November 1599, Malchi explained that "ever since she learned of Elizabeth, she had wanted to serve her, even though she is a Jew."[8] Safiye could not rescue Malchi and her son from the soldiers' wrath – or perhaps she chose not to.[9]

Sultan Mehmet III wanted to control his mother but could not. The best he could do was to request that she move from the New Palace to the Old Palace, but the move was short-lived.[10] She continued to enact her decisions by working in tandem with the chief of the white eunuchs in the harem.[11] She ruled practically unopposed for half a decade, appointing her allies to high posts and bringing down her foes. Mehmet's son, Mahmud, protested "how his father was altogether led by the old Sultana his Grandmother & the state went to ruin, she respecting nothing but her own desire to get money."[12] He often complained to his mother, whom the Valide Sultan disliked. Far from being a doting grandmother, Safiye saw to it that her ungrateful grandson was strangled to death. She informed Sultan Mehmet III that a sinister seer had foretold his imminent death. Suspecting a plot, he had his son executed in 1603, shortly before dying himself.

Mehmet III's other son, Ahmed, made sure that Safiye's influence was neutralized as soon as he took the throne. From Friday, January 9, 1604, the Valide Sultan was banished to the Old Palace but allowed to keep her stipend. Safiye seems to have lived on for more than a decade longer.

Safiye had four children with Murat, two sons and two daughters. All succeeding Ottoman sultans, down to the very last one in the twentieth century, descended from her. She too left her mark on the history of Islam.

# 13

# Tajul-Alam Safiatuddin Syah
## (1612–1675)

### DIAMONDS ARE NOT FOREVER

Sultana Tajul-Alam Safiatuddin Syah ruled as queen of the Sultanate of Aceh Darussalam for thirty-four years, 1641–1675. She held her own as she handled not only the demands of foreign diplomats and merchants, but also the fractious elite of her realm. While most coastal rulers in Java and Sumatra, in south-east Asia, capitulated to colonial manipulation, Tajul-Alam kept Aceh independent.

The hot, humid and tropically lush Aceh occupies the northern tip of the gigantic Island of Sumatra, which is now a province in the Republic of Indonesia – the most populous Muslim country in the world. On the west, north west and south west, Sumatra borders the Indian Ocean. The narrow Strait of Malacca separates it from the Malay Peninsula on the north east, and Java lies to the south east.

Hundreds of years before Tajul-Alam was born, Muslim merchants from India had gained a foothold in Sumatra, Java and the Malay Peninsula. Later geographers referred to this vast area as Further India, and later as the East Indies. Even before the arrival of Muslim traders in the thirteenth century, sea trade between China and the region thrived. The Venetian adventurer

Marco Polo, who passed through the region (though not Aceh proper) in 1292 on his way home from China, described the population as "for the most part idolaters, but many of those who dwell in the seaport towns have been converted to the religion of Mahomet, by the Saracen merchants who constantly frequent them."[1] Half a century after this observation, when the North African traveler Ibn Battuta arrived in the area on his way to China, he praised the local ruler as a good Muslim.

The Sultanate of Aceh Darussalam took shape in the name of Islam at the turn of the sixteenth century. The idealized description of the Sultanate as Darussalam, which means the "Abode of Peace," alludes to verses in the Quran: "God calls to the Abode of Peace, guiding whomever He wills to a straight path" and "They are bound to have an Abode of Peace in the presence of their Lord."[2] Both verses refer to the fulfillment of a divine promise in Paradise, in the Hereafter. Creating an earthly reflection of that heavenly abode was an aspiration in politics no less than in personal life. Among Muslim cities, the epithet belonged first and foremost to Baghdad, before the Mongols laid that once glorious city to waste. A new Abode of Peace soon flourished with its center at Banda Aceh, the Port of Aceh. Within a century, Muslim Sultans became the wealthiest and strongest kings across the East Indies. Year after year, more than a hundred ships called at the port, and long-distance trade in black pepper, silk, fragrant resin, gold and slaves brought the Sultanate unheard-of prosperity. Blending Islam with local customs, the Sultans of Aceh drew on diplomatic skill and military might to dominate lesser kingdoms in northern Sumatra, such as Daya, Pidie, Pasai, Aru and others.

In 1641, at the age of twenty-nine, Tajul-Alam succeeded to the throne of Aceh Darussalam, taking the title of Sultana. Sher Banu Khan's *Sovereign Women, Muslim Kingdom*, a detailed study of the Sultanas of Aceh, places Tajul-Alam's birth in the year 1612. Her father had named her Putri Sri Alam Permisuri in Malay, as well as giving her such nicknames as Tajul-Alam ("Crown of the World") and Safiatuddin ("Purely Faithful"). Almost nothing else, especially no personal detail, has reached us about this capable woman before she took the throne. Some historians claim that by the time Tajul-Alam became Sultana the Sultanate of Aceh Darussalam had just passed its prime. To some, the very fact that a twenty-nine-year-old widow ascended to the throne signaled a crisis in itself. The Sultanate had reached its greatest territorial extent under her father, who reigned from 1607 to 1637. However, his successor, Tajul-Alam's deceased husband, had failed to follow her father's good example. Instead, he ruled with an iron fist, nullifying or reversing many of the religious, economic and social policies that his father-in-law had enacted. His conduct during his reign from 1636 to 1641 alienated factions within the elite of his Sultanate. They had had enough of the haughty king's idiosyncrasies. So when he died unexpectedly at the age of thirty-one, for no apparent reason, his demise opened new opportunities for them.

Wealthy merchants, shipowners, shipyard operators and dock-masters, as well as high-ranking bureaucrats, held high stakes in the stability and prosperity of the Sultanate. As Aceh's elite, they formed the *orang-kaya*. In the Malay language, *orang-utan* – the reddish-brown arboreal great ape, or orangutan – literally means "man of the forest." By analogy, *orang-kaya* means "man of nobility" (or "men of nobility," since the singular and plural forms are the same). Today, the word simply means "rich" and may be applied to women as well as men.

Also invested in the fate of the Sultanate were the *ulama*, bearers and spokesmen of Islamic learning. Together, the *ulama* and the *orang-kaya* legitimated the rule of the Sultan. While the *orang-kaya* had their family roots in Aceh, most of the kingdom's *ulama* hailed from the outside, mainly India. The *orang-kaya* and the *ulama* belonged to different, scarcely overlapping, networks. Tajul-Alam's husband had alienated some in both groups. The *orang-kaya* and the *ulama* collectively agreed that his successor ought to act more fairly towards all factions in the realm.

When it came to succession, the Sultanate had no hard-and-fast rules. A suitable candidate had to be a native of Aceh and of royal birth, and had to demonstrate commitment to the principles of justice, as defined in Islamic terms and understood in Malay tradition or custom (*adat*). The fact that a woman, Nur Jahan, had effectively ruled over the Mughal Empire a few years earlier spoke volumes in favor of putting a woman on the throne in Aceh Darussalam. Mughal India provided a role model. Most of all, the choice depended on agreement among the various factions of the *orang-kaya* and the *ulama*. In principle, a woman could qualify. Although unprecedented in Aceh, rule by women had had precedents in Islamic history. No doubt choosing Tajul-Alam acknowledged her bloodline. Could she, like her father, bring wealth to Aceh Darussalam and restore its reputation, keeping both the *ulama* and the *orang-kaya* happy?

The seventeenth century marks a watershed moment in European colonialism. Having taken the lead in naval expansion into the "East" during the fifteenth and sixteenth centuries, the Portuguese had passed on the torch, reluctantly, to the more powerful armadas of the Dutch and the English. Like her predecessors in Aceh, as well as Hurra of Tétouan (of whom she had probably never heard), Tajul-Alam never liked the Portuguese. Vilifying them as religious enemies as well as foreign intruders, the Sultana was their irreconcilable enemy. Naturally, earlier Sultans of Aceh had allied themselves with fellow-Muslim Ottomans. The Ottomans had shared interests with Aceh as the main Muslim supplier of cargo from the Melaka Straits to the Mediterranean Sea, through the Red Sea. Half a century before Tajul-Alam's birth, one of her ancestors who ruled Aceh had reached out to the Ottoman Sultan Suleiman (r. 1520–1566) requesting naval support against the Portuguese. Now the Sultana forged alliances with the Dutch and the English as well.

The Dutch United East India Company (Veerinigde Ooost-Indische Compagnie, or VOC for short) and the English East India Company (EIC) escalated their interference in the affairs of the indigenous societies. In the first half of the seventeenth century both occupied local ports on the island of Java. The Dutch and the English christened their strongholds Batavia and Bantam respectively. Soon they took charge of most local affairs, but they failed to bring Aceh under control. Tajul-Alam's haughty predecessor had begun to undermine the economic independence of Aceh, and the Dutch sought to push this further. They had an opportunity to monopolize the supply and valuation of commodities by replacing other means of exchange with diamonds. However, the Sultana managed to block their efforts and maneuver out of crises, relying on the effective cooperation of the *orang-kaya*.

Calling it the "Jewels Affair," Sher Banu Khan illustrates how Tajul-Alam negotiated with the VOC. For almost four years, the Sultana drew on various mechanisms of compromise and competition to steer clear of troubled waters.[3]

Shortly after the Sultana ascended the throne, the VOC presented her with a large bill of unpaid expenses that her husband, the deceased king, had accrued. Yet another woman was held accountable for her husband's excess! They threatened that the honor of the kingdom, and the respect the Dutch had for her personally and as sovereign, depended on the reasonable settlement of this dispute. The timing seemed perfect and the rationale was clear for the Dutch: to pay them, the new and presumably insecure female ruler would either have to deplete her treasury or alternatively demand more taxes from the orang-kaya. The result in both cases would drive a wedge between her and the elite of the land. And, of course, the VOC would benefit.

The previous Sultan's extravagance was an open secret. Tajul-Alam's husband loved diamonds. He seemed to believe that ostentatious wealth reflected his power and therefore underscored his legitimacy as the Sultan. Not content with table-cut or point-cut diamonds, he ordered special designs through the VOC, demanding that the best craftsmen cut them for him in the Netherlands. The Sultan once commissioned a silken belt studded with custom-cut diamonds, woven in the same Persian style that the Mughals wore in India.

The Mughals displayed their power by using jewelry on their robes, their headgear, and their belts. The world-famous 191-carat Koh-i-Noor diamond that made its way to Britain and onto Queen Victoria's crown in the nineteenth century, seems to have come to Babur's attention some three centuries earlier. Possessing jewels and wearing them reflected political power. Perhaps by ordering a bejeweled belt made in the Persian-style of the Mughals, Tajul-Alam's husband wished to claim a basis of legitimacy for himself that reached to pre-Islamic times in Persia. He added a few more emerald and diamond pendants to his wish-list. At some point, he had a 900-kilogram throne made of gold,[4] which a VOC representative, Johan Truijtman, valued at 100,000 guilders. To highlight the estimated value of this throne, it is worth recalling that around the same time, thousands of kilometers away in New Amsterdam, agents of the West Dutch India Company had given the equivalent of sixty guilders to the Lenape people in exchange for ownership of the 22,000-acre Island of Manhattan.[5]

Sher Banu Khan provides details of a contemporary report made by the Dutch commissar Pieter Sourij. On July 12, 1641, he had his first audience with the Sultana, demanding nothing less than 15,000 taels for the jewels her husband had ordered. One week later, she ordered the *orang-kaya* and her jewelers to gather at her palace-interior, the *balai*, to appraise the jewels. Her eunuch, Maharaja Adonna Lilla, with the dock-owners and a couple of other *orang-kaya*, carefully examined them and suggested a price that outraged the company delegates. Instead of the requested 15,000, they offered 5,900 taels, and then agreed to add another 2,000 on top. The VOC liaison objected to such "frivolous talk," as he called it.

The tussle for an acceptable jewel price continued after that first meeting. Most of the *orang-kaya* agreed that the queen should pay, perhaps at a discount. A few opposed the purchase altogether. VOC officials tried their familiar ways of bribing and arm-twisting. Divided as they were, the *orang-kaya* wanted to maintain good relations with the Dutch, realizing the possible damage of going to war with the VOC. They also knew the importance of keeping the treasury healthy for the kingdom's stability. Nearly all of them wanted the Sultana to continue in the tradition of her illustrious father and uphold friendship with the Dutch. The Sultana's eunuch, a close confidant and a highly influential member of the *orang-kaya*, raised the offer to 9,000 taels but complained that he was offering more than he should and that some of the big stones that the Dutch had brought were worth "no more than pebbles." Sourij informed them of the possibility of lowering their asking price in Persia from 15,000 to 12,000–13,000 taels. The *orang-kaya* would prefer to pay no more than 9000. Eventually, both sides settled for 10,000 taels. To pay for the jewels, the Sultana ordered a reduction of 4,000 taels in the tolls that Dutch ships had to pay, and that the balance of 6,000 taels should be spread over two monsoon seasons, called *mousams* in Malay.

To celebrate and add some levity at the end of the prolonged and sometimes frustrating negotiations, Tajul-Alam asked for a small favor. She wanted to see the Dutch negotiators "honor" her by dancing for her and her other women councilors. To display their appreciation, the VOC officials obliged. Sher Banu Khan tells us that the chief negotiator reported back to Holland that watching their hops and bounces, onlookers had filled the court with their guffaws of laughter and had been exceptionally amused.

Tajul-Alam's handling of the "Jewels Affair" hints at a lot more than her bargaining skills in purchasing diamonds at a discounted price. The VOC pushed for setting a standard for exchange in precious stones, primarily diamonds, whose supply and valuation they exclusively controlled. Diamond cutting was a specialty of the Low Countries, especially the Netherlands, where exact tools and techniques had been developed. The Sultana and her orang-kaya set the terms with VOC agents, negotiating the quantity of diamonds and gems needed in Aceh and their price, as well as the payment plan. This was nothing less than an act of independent diplomacy. In carrying it out, Tajul-Alam broke with the royal habit of intimidating the *orang-kaya* and fighting wars with outsiders. Instead, with the cooperation of the *orang-kaya*, she negotiated workable relationships with foreign rivals and enemies.

Sher Banu Khan emphasizes how the Sultana of Aceh pushed for more collaborative, institutionally stable and economically pragmatic ways of protecting private property, promoting security and improving the welfare of her subjects. Again, the "Jewels Affair" illustrates that, unlike her predecessors, Tajul-Alam did not rely on military might, the emasculation of the *orang-kaya*, or the ostentation of diamond belts and golden thrones as a basis for legitimacy.

The shift from brute force to negotiation under Sultana Tajul-Alam had a religious basis. Capitalizing on justice, peace and ethical conduct as hallmarks of Islamic rule, she moved away from emphasizing strict adherence to the letter of formalistic definitions of Islamic piety. Unlike her husband, she withdrew patronage from those members of the *ulama* who failed to connect with the *orang-kaya* and the local population by their relentless criticism of what they denigrated as un-Islamic in Acehnese traditions and customs. Her predecessors had often supported those *ulama*, partly out of religious conviction and partly as a form of insurance against the *orang-kaya*.

In 1637 Tajul-Alam's deceased husband had brought a scholar of Islamic sharia, or law, Sheikh Nur-al-Din Raniri (d. 1658), to Aceh. Originally from what is now Gujarat in India, Sheikh Raniri pioneered sharia-writing in Malay and soon raised the profile of the Sultanate of Aceh Darussalam as a center of Islamic learning. His most notable work, a multi-volume compilation in Malay, set a new standard for Muslim belief and practice in that region. However, finding the new female sovereign unappreciative of his work, Raniri left Aceh for good in 1644.

In accord with the current of her times, Tajul-Alam preferred a more conciliatory and inclusive vision of Islam. In the middle of the sixteenth century, the philosophical world view of the Andalusian Sufi thinker Ibn Arabi (1165–1240) had struck roots in India, and more broadly in Aceh across the East Indies as well. Its most articulate regional advocate, Hamza Pansuri (ca. 1535–1590), acknowledged as the first great poet in the Malay language, wrote extensively on God, man and existence.

At the time, Ibn Arabi's philosophy was enjoying a prolonged heyday in Ottoman lands, Safavid Iran, as well as Mughal India. These teachings are commonly, but inaccurately labeled as pantheistic. This vague label conceals the subtleties and complexities involved in Ibn Arabi's thinking. Ibn Arabi slides over such differences as language, skin color and even religion to emphasize the essential unity of all. In embracing Ibn Arabi's teachings, the Sultana found herself in good intellectual company, alongside the enlightened Mughal prince Dara Shikuh (1615–1659). The three female sovereigns who succeeded Tajul-Alam to the throne in Aceh Darussalam continued to bolster specific concepts of Muslim piety and authority that differed from those advocated by some of the *ulama*, in Aceh and beyond. As seen elsewhere and in various other contexts, such intellectual debates complemented, or rather mirrored, conflicts between factions in and outside the court.

Eventually the *ulama* came back and with a vengeance. The renewed empowerment of the sharia-based outlook in Aceh reflected developments in Mughal India under the strict monarch Aurangzeb (1658–1707). Once again men brought this hadith to the fore: "Those who entrust their affairs to a woman will never know prosperity."[6]

Clearly, two visions of Islam contended with each other. A backlash against Ibn Arabi's teachings that first arose in Istanbul, Isfahan and Delhi eventually arrived on the shores of Aceh. It brought the rule of women to an end.

# 14

# Tahereh
## (ca. 1814–1852)

## HEROINE OR HERETIC?

The dawn of modernity at the beginning of the nineteenth century produced a new complex of political, economic, and religious challenges, conflicts and controversies for Muslims as for everyone else. Tahereh (ca. 1814–1852) lived in those extraordinary times and left an extraordinary legacy of her own. Some denounce her as an apostate; others celebrate her as a saint. To this day her story remains entangled with religious controversies from nineteenth-century Iran.

Tahereh was born in or around 1814 in the Iranian city of Qazvin. Her father named her Fatemeh; the name of the Prophet's beloved daughter that was and remains highly popular among Shia Muslims. He also gave her the byname of Zarrin-Taj, "the girl with a golden crest." The name Tahereh, used here, is one of the handful of names and titles she received throughout her short life.

Qazvin, once the Safavid capital in the sixteenth century, remained a bastion of Shia Islam during the nineteenth century. The Safavids had gone, and after a lull of a few decades a new dynasty had taken over – the Qajars, who now ruled from Tehran. A mere hundred miles away from the new capital, Qazvin still thrived as a center of commerce and a citadel of religious learning. As Shia religious scholars, or *ulama*, Tahereh's family upheld Qazvin's reputation as "the Abode of the Faithful."

At the time of Tahereh's birth, a momentous debate divided the faithful living in Qazvin, especially within the ranks of the *ulama*. Her family was deeply involved. The controversy centred on the proper way of leading a faithful life as a Shia Muslim in a rapidly changing cultural milieu. So long as Prophet Muhammad lived and delivered the divine message, his conduct had clarified the meaning and implications of faith. According to the form of Shia Islam practiced in Iran, after the Prophet the twelve Imams continued to deliver divine law. Their statements and actions were infallible. However, the twelfth Imam, called the Mahdi, had gone into occultation (become hidden from view) as far back as the ninth century CE, and was to return at the end of time. Who spoke for God in his absence? At the turn of the nineteenth century the question had acquired new urgency, if only because society seemed to be changing as never before.

In Tahereh's town, one side of the debate stressed the necessity of centralizing religious authority. To have faith and to live faithfully meant following in the footsteps of living exemplars of faith who knew the law of God: how to pray; how to fast; what to eat and not eat; and what professions to choose and which ones to abandon. For everything in life there had to be a ruling that the faithful ought to follow. The advocates of this view called for the training of a hierarchy of specialists in foundational matters, or *osul*. This was known as the Osuli position. Solid training in the fundamentals of how to live paved the way for exercising expert reasoning, or *ijtihad*, in working out the details of divine law. Anyone who could complete the training to the highest level would become a *mojtahed*. The Osuli or pro-*mojtahed* position presented the faithful with a choice: either become a *mojtahed* yourself or follow one. The masses had a religious duty to follow the *mojtahed*s, who would shoulder the responsibility of speaking for God.

Those on the other side of the debate rejected the reduction of faith to such a framework. To follow opinions formulated by fallible men – how could this be the essence of faith? No matter how well trained, men were still fallible, and regardless of how informed their opinions might be, how could they have the authority to speak for God? The Osulis belittled their rivals by calling them Akhbaris, implying that all they had to stand on amounted to *akhbar*, reports about the sayings and doings of the Prophet and the Imams. In short, the Osulis extended religious authority to learned experts, and the opposition did not.

In keeping with the custom of the Qajar era of reverence for the *ulama*, Tahereh's family were respected pillars of the community in Qazvin. However, her parents came from opposite sides of the ongoing Osuli-Akhbari dispute. Her father and his formidable older brother were exponents of the Osuli position. Her mother's side of the family belonged in the other camp. Tahereh's life was shaped by the conflict dividing her family.

Growing up in an *ulama* family, Tahereh enjoyed the privilege of taking formal lessons at home. From an early age she learned what suited a respectable Shia female. Her father taught her the Quran and hadith. Her mother, Amineh, an educated woman in her own right, recited poems to her, helped her memorize many others and taught her to write selected ones with a reed pen. At home and at the madrasa, Tahereh learned to speak and write in Persian, Azeri and Arabic. She went on to attend lessons outside her home at the madrasa that her father had established.

Founded in the same year that Tahereh was born or shortly after, her father's madrasa had a solid reputation and hundreds of students. Here she sat at the feet of her paternal uncle to learn Islamic law and jurisprudence. Meanwhile, Tahereh's brothers and cousins introduced her to the labyrinths of Shia philosophical thought. She was a quick student. Her older brother once remarked:

All of us, her brothers and cousins, feared speaking in her presence, so much did her knowledge intimidate us. Should we hazard to propose an opinion, she would demonstrate where we went wrong, always arguing clearly, rigorously, and in a magisterial manner that bewildered us and made us withdraw.[1]

Seeing Tahereh's brilliance, her father wished, "Would that she had been a boy, to illuminate my legacy and to succeed me!"[2] Much to his chagrin, he soon realized that she had no interest in succeeding him. Instead, she wished to overthrow whatever he advocated. Ill-placed expectations cost both father and daughter dearly. Tahereh felt closer to the vision of religious life on her mother's side of the family.

Tahereh was still a child when the religious crisis escalated, with the arrival in Qazvin of a notable opponent of the *mojtaheds*. Beginning in the middle of the 1810s, probably from 1812, the charismatic Shaykh Ahmad Ahsaie (1753–1826) had traveled to Iran from Ahsa, a Shia-populated region on the north eastern fringe of the Arabian Peninsula, now known for having the largest crude oil reserves in the world. This man of enormous learning and piety outmatched most *mojtaheds* in the sophistication of his thought and speech, and the quality – and quantity – of his writing. He agreed with the Akhbaris that imitating another fallible person failed to guarantee salvation. He insisted that religious truth could only be discovered by coming into direct contact with its source. He emphasized the need for spiritual exercises in order to draw ever closer to the spirit of the Fourteen Infallibles: that is, the Prophet, his daughter Fatima, and the twelve Imams. One of his teachings was that through devotion one could enter the presence of the twelfth, or hidden, Imam on the spiritual plane.

Shaykh Ahmad won over followers and sympathizers in town after town, calling for a radical revision of religious thought and practice. The Shaykh's followers were called Shaykhis, and several individuals on Tahereh's mother's side of the family had become Shaykhis. In fact, it was her maternal uncle who invited the Shaykh to Qazvin in 1822 and then arranged for him to lead public prayers at the town's congregational mosque. Tahereh's mother had studied with Shaykh Ahmad at the family madrasa that her own brother had founded.

This welcoming of the *mojtaheds*' arch nemesis to Qazvin unnerved Tahereh's uncle, her father's brother, himself a *mojtahed*. Wielding his authority, he denounced Shaykh Ahmad, branding him a blasphemer and forcing him to leave town in 1824. Tahereh's mother's side of the family took the brunt of this assault on their leader. A couple of years later, the Shaykh, Tahereh's paternal uncle added his voice to the chorus of *mojtaheds* declaring the military confrontation between Iranian and Russian troops a religious war, and making it a religious duty for all Muslim men to participate in the fight against the Russian army of unbelievers. Some historians hold the *mojtaheds* as culpable as the Qajar royal house for what proved to be a disgraceful failure. The Russo-Persian Wars of the early nineteenth century resulted in huge territorial losses for Iran, including what is now Georgia, Armenia, Dagestan and Azerbaijan in the Caucasus. In the final round of these ill-fated wars, 1826–1828, Tahereh lost her beloved sixteen-year-old brother, Mohammad.

Even as a young girl Tahereh could sense how denouncing Shaykh Ahmad and supporting the Qajar war effort benefited her eldest paternal uncle. These and other displays of religious authority brought him abundant wealth, respect and influence. She regarded him as a man of the world, not a man of God like Shaykh Ahmad. Her father disapproved of any such assessment of his older brother. He had tried to keep to the middle ground but when it came to the war against Russia, he had supported it. So when Tahereh opened up her heart to her father one night, saying how she had "thirsted after the teachings of Shaykh Ahmad and . . . yearned for his explanations, and those inner truths," he shut her up, lambasting her for turning into "a lost soul."

To "save" Tahereh, who was aged between fourteen and seventeen, her father and his brother married her off. The groom, who was none other than the equally self-important elder son of her uncle, soon took her to Karbala, an important Shia shrine city in Iraq and a stronghold of *mojtaheds*. Karbala became the couple's home for over a decade. They had three children together, two sons and a daughter. Their marriage was an unhappy one. Soon after they returned to Qazvin in 1841, Tahereh left him and moved into her father's house with her children. Within two years, she got a divorce.

Intellectually curious as ever, Tahereh initiated a correspondence with the leading Shaykhi authority in Karbala. She had heard about him during her years there and now sought spiritual advice from him. She candidly wrote of her longing to witness the coming of the twelfth Imam, the Mahdi. Much to her delight, this man did not dismiss her queries, unlike her father and perhaps her former husband. Endearingly addressing the unseen petitioner as the "Solace of the Eyes" (*qurrat-al-'ayn*), he assured her that the advent of the Mahdi was nigh.

So Tahereh packed up and left for Karbala, taking her daughter and younger sister with her. A couple of male relatives accompanied them for safety. Upon her arrival, in January 1844, she learned that her letter-writing mentor had died just a few weeks earlier. His widow introduced her to the circle of the man's closest disciples and she joined them in days-long fasting, lengthy engagement in prayer and other spiritual exercises. They all awaited the advent of the Mahdi.

One night, in a dream-vision, Tahereh encountered a young Seyed – a descendent of the Prophet – and described him to the other disciples of the deceased Shaykhi leader in Karbala. Was this the man who would lead them to Mahdi, the Lord of the Age? The men went out in search of him. They were looking for the Bab, "the gate," to the realm of the hidden twelfth Imam. Although she could not ride out freely with the men in that circle of disciples, Tahereh made her presence felt in writing. She addressed a letter to the Bab and sent it with her fellow spiritual seekers. The men eventually encountered a young Seyed in the city of Shiraz, whom they identified as the divinely chosen guide they had sought. By virtue of that letter, Tahereh became a member of the initial nucleus of the Bab's followers – the Babis.

The Bab was miraculously prolific. He produced more writings in one night than most writers made available in months or years. Soon the lines blurred: for the Babis, what began as recognizing the Bab as a *guide* to the messiah turned into an acceptance that he *was* himself the messiah.

Some Babis devoted themselves to a militant preparing of the way for the messianic prelude to the final Day of Judgment. In 1844 exactly one thousand lunar years would have passed since the occultation of the Mahdi. Envisioning an apocalyptic battle between the forces of good and evil, the Babis proceeded to Karbala, awaiting their turn to join the armies of good.

To put an end to any such displays of militancy, the Qajar court detained the Bab and incarcerated him in a fortress, far away from the reach of the Babis. This action failed to deter most Babis.

As a woman, Tahereh did not join her fellow Babis on the battleground. Instead, she wrote and lectured, both in Persian and Arabic, composing and reciting her own poems expressing mystical ideals. Dedicating herself to expounding the words of the Bab, she quickly realized their spiritual, intellectual and institutional implications. To declare that immediate contact with the Mahdi was now at hand resolved the Shaykhi tension between finding the Mahdi inside one's heart and seeking him in the outside world. It also dispensed with the *mojtaheds* as fallible spokesmen of the divine. Tahereh pushed for an even more radical position, declaring in 1846 that received religious law had ceased to be applicable. This sounded nothing less than blasphemous.

The Muslim *ulama* in Karbala, Sunnis as well as Shias, condemned the Babis as dangerous heretics. Taking their cue from their religious leaders, the general public protested against the presence of the Babis in the sacred shrine city. They pelted the door of Tahereh's home, and increasing pressure made it impossible for her to stay there. After a few months the townspeople had her expelled.

Entering Baghdad around February 1847, Tahereh stayed with the city's most powerful Sunni clan. The local authorities had probably made this arrangement both to keep this Persian subject safe and to decide what had caused her trouble in Karbala. Her host, a renowned religious authority in the city, engaged her in dialogue, posing questions and weighing her answers. Two or three months later, higher authorities ordered her to return to Iran.

After a long journey on a treacherous road, Tahereh received a cold reception in Qazvin. Her estranged husband and his unforgiving father did all they could to make her feel unwelcome. On top of his criticism of the Shaykhis, the uncle rejected the Babi beliefs in even harsher terms. However unsympathetic he also was to the Babi cause, Tahereh's father never wavered in shielding his daughter. At one meeting, the neighborhood *ulama* taunted him by mocking his daughter. One of the men crudely said, "No honor comes to a house where the hens crow, not the roosters." In nineteenth-century Iran, where honor was valued so highly, such a snide remark made him weep, and he got up and left without a word.

The family feud took a tragic turn. On October 25, 1847, a man stabbed Tahereh's paternal uncle in the middle of the prayer before dawn. The elderly *mojtahed* died of his injuries. The blame fell on the Babis and fingers pointed at Tahereh. Fellow Babis helped her move back to Tehran. She kept a low profile in the capital, but continued to give sermons, sometimes from behind a veil to male visitors.

When the ruling monarch died in 1848, the Babis saw an opportunity to regroup and gain ground. Tahereh joined the Babi congregation in Badasht, an open field located about a day's ride from Tehran. There she appeared in public without a veil, displaying her commitment to the suspension – what the Babis called the abrogation – of existing Islamic law. Her action struck panic among the onlookers. How could a woman dare to unveil herself in public? Some Babis fled and some renounced their faith in the Bab. Others stood fast.

From Badasht and elsewhere across Iran, hundreds of Babis went on to the Fort of Tabarsi in northern Iran. Accounts of what really happened vary drastically. Conflict broke out between the Babis and pro-government forces, both locals and those sent over from the capital. The war dragged on for two years and ended with the Babis being routed. To quash further insurgency, the Qajar court had the Bab executed. Back in Tehran, Tahereh was placed under detention. But still women crowded to see and listen to her, spellbound by her words.

Then came an attempt on the life of the new monarch. On August 15, 1852 a Babi shot a pistol at the king. As with many attempts at political assassination, it is difficult to determine who exactly was behind him. There is good reason to believe that the young monarch's cousins had an interest in seeing him killed. Be that as it may, government authorities not only killed the assailant instantly but also launched a wholesale massacre of the Babis in Tehran. Perhaps ordered by the royal court, but more likely on the initiative of the city's headman or even lower authorities, henchmen dragged Tahereh into a garden one night in late August 1852. Forcing her scarf down her throat, they choked her to death then flung her body into a well. Having sided with the Qajar court, the *mojtaheds* were delighted to see the downfall of the Babis. When it came to Tahereh, detractors leveled the most vulgar accusations against her, often adding salacious details to the unveiling incident in Badasht. In response, the Babis pointed to the name the Bab himself had given her: Tahereh the

Immaculate. The Sunni scholar who had sheltered Tahereh in Baghdad refuted the insinuations: "I saw in her such virtues that I have not seen in most men. She was intelligent and cultured and unique in her virtue and chastity."[3] Her own daughter and son later bore witness that their mother had spent her last days reciting the Quran and performing daily prayers, like a good Muslim.[4]

Some historians celebrate Tahereh as an icon of the women's movement in Iran. Others, perhaps emboldened by self-righteousness or feeling threatened by Tahereh's prodigious abilities as a thinker and speaker, have besmirched her honor, questioned her character and even accused her of plagiarizing her poems. Contrasting images of Tahereh have lingered: a saintly heroine, a dangerous heretic. She lived at a time when Iran, the heartland of Shia Islam, was facing the complex concept of modernity. The urgent question of the time was to decide who speaks for religion; and, no less, what religion has to say.

# 15

# Nana Asmau
## (1793–1864)

## Jihad and Sisterhood

Encounters with modernity in Africa bore some similarity to those in Iran, India, and the Ottoman lands, but also showed distinctive regional factors.

The Fulani Jihad at the turn of the nineteenth century redirected the course of Islam in Africa. The war and the religious force that propelled it changed the political landscape of West Africa. The status of women also changed as a result. A female teacher and healer took on a leading role in empowering women during and after the war. We know this woman of legendary capability as Nana Asmau (1793–1864). Her contemporaries called her Uwar Gari – "Mother of All."

Born in 1793, Nana Asmau was the twenty-second or twenty-third of the forty or so children of Shehu Usman dan Fodio (1754–1817). Nana was an honorific title she received later in life. While she was still a child, her father came under pressure from local rulers for his advocacy of Islamic values in their native village of Degel. In 1803 she left home with the rest of her family when her father led them and hundreds of devoted followers into the shrublands of West Africa. That exodus changed her life for good. The uprising that ensued is known as the Fulani Jihad.

It all began in Degel, an oasis in Hausa-land. The Hausa people (plural Hausawa), who still comprise a large ethnic group in Africa, primarily claimed what is now northern Nigeria and Niger as Hausa-land. Unlike the people living in the many nondescript hamlets that dotted the landscape at the turn of the nineteenth century, most of the inhabitants of Degel came from the outside, as did Shehu Usman dan Fodio. In 1774, two decades before fathering Nana Asmau, he arrived in Degel and dedicated himself to building a model community centered on Islamic learning and virtues. The village of Degel may have predated Shehu Usman's arrival, but he made it live up to the meaning of its name, which in the local vernacular meant "righteous." Usman envisioned it as a haven for its inhabitants, enabling them to avoid worldly distractions and focus on the cultivation of piety, learning and spiritual values. Shehu Usman brought both the vision and the determination to realize it. From Degel, he ventured out to preach to the herdsmen, weavers, butter-makers and others in Hausa-land. He warned them that the Muslim community, the *umma*, had veered far away from the original teachings of the Quran and the Prophet Muhammad. Asmau grew up hearing her father's clarion call for the revival of the exemplary conduct of the Prophet, the *sunna*:

> [The Prophet] patched his own garments and mended his own footwear. He performed his own chores, personally giving fodder to his water-bearing camel. He carried his own goods from the market, never allowing anyone else to do that for him.[1]

People listened to Shehu Usman as he traveled across Hausa-land. Besides knowledge of Islam, he had charisma, an air of spiritual potency or *baraka* about him. Like most Muslim leaders in African history, he combined the double virtues of *baraka* and book learning, embodying the Sufi ethos.

Islam has deep roots in West Africa. As far back as the ninth or tenth century, traveling merchants tried to unite West Africa with Muslim societies in the north. Right up to the middle of the twelfth century the Fatimid caliphate supported such efforts at unification spreading unified beliefs and practices among the people helped to link regional networks of commerce. By the twelfth century Islam had a firm footing in West Africa's Sahel and savannah regions. Then the Sufis arrived on the heels of Mongol invasions. Many came from as far east as present-day Iran and Afghanistan, escaping from the scourge that had laid their homelands to waste. By the late thirteenth century, Timbuktu, Gao and Kano, all in present-day Mali, had become bastions of Islamic learning. The prosperity of those cities derived from trade in gold, copper, cloth, leather, salt and grain. West African Muslims joined the rest of the Muslim commonwealth in the annual pilgrimage or Hajj to Mecca and Medina. One such pilgrim, King Mansa Mousa of Mali, stunned onlookers in the mid-1320s with his glittering treasures, especially his seemingly inexhaustible supply of gold. Hajj caravans brought books back to West Africa as souvenirs. For generations owning books reflected social status. From Mali, Islamic teachings arrived in Hausa-land by the fourteenth century. Five centuries later, Nana could easily access books that had arrived in Degel from Timbuktu, Tripoli and Cairo.

Also centuries before Nana Asmau's time, forces of European colonialism had penetrated West Africa, opening a new front in the heat of the *Reconquista*. Landing on West African shores from the north, Portuguese and Spanish soldiers of the cross incited regional feuds. As a deliberate policy, they fueled violence among local Muslim and non-Muslim chieftaincies. Arming non-Muslims with firearms, they mobilized mercenary revolts. These interventions helped to unleash the horrors of the trans-atlantic slave trade. Over the course of the next four centuries, more than four million slaves were shipped from West African ports to Europe and the Americas. Hundreds of thousands among them were Muslim. Nana Asmau's efforts at reorienting women's lives in Hausa-land unfolded against this backdrop.

Shehu Usman condemned the practice of capturing and selling slaves, not least Muslim slaves, to the Europeans. Objecting to this as yet another way people were leaving the right path, he criticized his contemporaries in Hausa-land for failing to follow the exemplary conduct of the Prophet. He called them to a life of strict moral discipline. However, the ruler of Degel had no patience for hearing about the plight of the slaves, the hardships of the poor and the Muslim duty to give alms. He rejected reminders of the Prophet Muhammad's humility and charitable conduct. To him, such talk sounded like an effort to incite sedition. Alarmed by the number and devotion of those around Shehu Usman, the ruler forbad him from preaching and then, wary of the charismatic preacher's activities, decided to banish him. This decision backfired and opened a new chapter in Nana Asmau's life.

An army of men rallied to support Shehu Usman against the ruler of Degel. Most of Usman's backers were Hausa-land nomads called Fulanis, and so his uprising is known as the Fulani Jihad. As war raged on, from February 1804 to October 1808, thousands of men fell in battle, and thousands more women and children suffered. The young Nana Asmau participated in the war effort. Hardship molded her identity and character and helped her to bond with her father's flock. She witnessed the planning and execution of war first-hand, enduring the same torments. For months women and children wandered in the wilderness. They huddled together in ramshackle camps. Often at the point of starvation, they lived in fear of being assaulted by enemy men as well as the wild beasts of the savannah. Shared suffering bonded Nana Asmau and other survivors for life.

Eventually, Shehu Usman dan Fodio prevailed. He established a new caliphate, based at the Fulani stronghold of Sokoto, near the confluence of the Rima and the Sokoto rivers. As leader, he took on the title of Caliph, Sultan, and Commander of the Faithful. Nana Asmau played a central role in the caliphate. From 1808 until the end of her life in 1864, she saw her father, brother, nephew and grandnephew rule as caliphs. Her husband, whom she married at the age of fifteen, also had a hand in building the Sokoto caliphate.

Nana Asmau felt the urgency of healing the wounds of her war-stricken community. Men killed in battle had left behind widows and orphans. What should be done about the thousands of boys, girls and women captured from the enemy? What was their status? Slaves? Almost every house had them as concubines – Nana Asmau's brother, who soon after the war succeeded their father as caliph, had taken in several. How could these women be integrated into the community? Shehu Usman dan Fodio always stressed the Islamic virtue of showing compassion to the defeated and treating widows and orphans charitably. His daughter Asmau used education to do just that.

Raised by strong, loving women himself, Shehu Usman felt secure in their company. He had learned to read and write sitting at the feet of his mother and grandmother, both of whom were literate and wrote poetry. He insisted on the empowerment of the women of the Sokoto caliphate. The following passage illustrates how strongly he expressed his view on this:

> [These men] condemn their wives, daughters, and female relatives to a vegetative life, like animals. They mistreat them like pots and pans, and once broken after long use toss them on a dung-heap. This is a travesty.[2]

His daughter took this teaching to heart. Like her father, she saw women playing a larger part in community affairs, beyond their traditional roles of cooking, cleaning and performing similar domestic duties. Asmau came from a line of literate and learned women, and had been nurtured as such by three of her father's co-wives. When her brother succeeded their father as caliph, she had a chance to influence policy.

According to local tradition, the sister of the ruler enjoyed an elevated status in Hausa-land. Capitalizing on that, Nana Asmau committed herself to bettering the life of the women of the Sokoto caliphate. She had her work cut out. Focusing on education as the primary means of empowerment, she taught women about Islam, about the Quran and the teachings of the Prophet. She pressed the point that the mistreatment and debasement of women contradicted the exemplary conduct of Prophet Muhammad. To her, reviving the roots of pure Islam depended on raising the status of women. The time had come to uproot degrading views and unwholesome practices against women. Like her father, she blamed some jurists or ulama for introducing such notions, which others had then adopted in ignorance. Her concern was not removing the veil or calling for women to mingle freely with men. She wanted women to know more about the teachings of Islam; to read, write, sing and work. That would set them free from ignorance. She measured freedom in terms of acquiring and applying knowledge of Islam. She gave them moral lessons from the life of the Prophet and his companions; instructed them on the basics of the law, including matters of diet and personal hygiene; and taught them traditional remedies for healing both body and soul.

Reaching out to her people in all their diversity, Nana Asmau wrote and taught in four languages: Arabic, the standard medium for religious learning and liturgy; Hausa, which was dominant in Hausa-land; Fulani or Fulfulde, her mother tongue; and to a lesser extent Tamasheq, another local vernacular. She wrote works in prose as well as verse, many of which reveal her familiarity with the Islamic tradition. She felt free to adapt material from others, and frequently cited passages from the Quran. Her didactic verse outlined what to wear, how to behave, what to eat and what to believe. In straightforward terms, she sought to foster a fear of God as she emphasized the importance of maintaining pious conduct, avoiding the vicissitudes of worldly life, and following the teachings of Islam.

In a work entitled *Sufi Women*, Nana Asmau named several contemporary women as exemplars for her students to revere and follow. A Sufi herself, Nana Asmau was regarded as blessed with spiritual potency, or *baraka*. People said that when her brother had found himself in difficulties in battle during the Fulani War, she had thrown him a torch which he had used to burn down his enemy's camp. However, *baraka* had to be differentiated from what was called *bori*. While *baraka* was associated with Islam and highly esteemed, *bori* was condemned as evil. In Hausa language, *bori* is a spiritual force or spirit that resides in all things.

Non-Muslims in Hausa-land held *bori*-related rituals that involved dancing, drumming, drinking, calabash-rapping and the use of effigies. Some occult arts and magic acts, called *boko*, surrounded these rites and were used, for example, to heal infertility or cure illnesses attributed to demon-possession. Women played a central role in these rites, some of which are still practiced in Hausa-land. Looking down on *bori* and *boko* as blatant remnants of the dark age of disbelief, or *jahiliya*, Nana Asmau aimed to eradicate people's interest in them. She composed a book, in Arabic prose, drawing on verses from the Quran and sayings attributed to the Prophet to prescribe proper ways to cure illness, ease pain, treat wounds, ward off the evil eye and so forth.

Few women were literate at the time. So Nana Asmau's verses were primarily meant to be memorized and recited. Women especially would chant and sing them at home and in the open fields. Besides enriching the oral repertoire, she also wrote for the literate elite of the Sokoto caliphate.

Men as well as women respected her as a *malama*, a word that combines the meaning of a woman teacher, healer and leader. She dispensed what the people needed: knowledge of Islam, instructions on dos and don'ts, and a sense of spirituality. Women flocked to her home from other villages to sit at her feet and take lessons. Those among them who could write recorded her words on their wooden tablets or *allo*s. People called these women the Yan Taru, or Associates. Each group of the Yan Taru had a leader of its own, a *jaji*. In an initiation ceremony, each *jaji* received a red strip of cloth and a large, balloon-shaped grass hat, a *malfa*. These women carried their emblems of religious authority, and their learning, back to their villages, with soldiers of the Sokoto caliphate protecting them on their journey both ways.

Nana Asmau's reputation extended beyond the Sokoto caliphate. She had contacts in the greater part of the Sahel and western Sudanic Africa, including Morocco and Mauritania. Her legacy lives on in the twenty-first century, not only in her home-land, which is now Nigeria, but elsewhere in the world. Singers sometimes set her poems to music.

Today, Nigeria is officially a secular democratic republic. Sometimes called the Giant of Africa, this nation of 190 million people has the largest population of any country in Africa, a population split almost equally between Muslims and Christians. The first Christian missions seen in what is now southern Nigeria during the 1840s coincided with the most productive years of Nana Asmau's activity in the north. Subsequently, Christianity enjoyed phenomenal growth in the heat of the so-called Scramble for Africa, the race among the Christian rulers of Europe to occupy and colonize the African continent from the 1880s to the outbreak of the First World War. Eventually the colonial officers of the British crown abolished the Sokoto caliphate in 1903. The space that Nana Asmau and her associates had carved out for women's active presence in social life disappeared.

When Nana Asmau died in 1864, her body was laid to rest near that of her father. The site, called Hubbare in Hausa, is now a place of pilgrimage. Hundreds of visitors come daily from Nigeria, Sudan, Senegal and elsewhere. Her legacy lives on. Her sister Maryam, niece Tamodi, and then others continued to oversee an organization centered on her lessons. Today women still journey to Sokoto from as far away as Europe and North America, chanting and singing lines from Nana Asmau's poetry. Some follow a rigorous curriculum, taking lessons in Arabic, Quran interpretation, law and doctrine.

A caliphate existed in Nigeria two centuries before Boko Haram shocked the world with violent calls for the establishment of one. At the peak of its power, the Sokoto caliphate ruled over an area that today extends across the borders of Burkina Faso, Benin, Nigeria, Niger, Chad and Cameroon. Whereas in 2016 Boko Haram terrorized communities in the name of Islam, kidnapping schoolgirls and forcing women into slavery, back in the nineteenth century the Sokoto caliphate empowered women through education. Boko Haram in West Africa and similar organizations across the globe falsify the Islamic past at every turn.

# 16

# Mukhlisa Bubi
## (1869–1937)

### Educator and Jurist

The course of modernity in the Russian Empire affected the history of Islam in decisive ways, especially during the late nineteenth century and the first half of the twentieth. Mukhlisa Bubi, a leading Muslim educator and pioneering female jurist, lived at that time. Her ghost has returned, and with a vengeance. As recently as 2014 women's organizations celebrated her in Kazan, the capital of the Russian Republic of Tatarstan. They proclaimed Mukhlisa a pioneering educator and jurist, and an exemplary model for contemporary Muslim women.

Mukhlisa was still a young woman when she championed the cause of modern education for Muslim girls in nineteenth-century Russia. Later, she became the first Muslim woman judge in modern history. She dedicated the last ten years of her life to promulgating laws and regulations for the advancement of women's rights. Eventually, she met a tragic end during the anti-religious campaigns of the Union of Soviet Socialist Republics (USSR).

Mukhlisa was born in 1869 in Tatarstan, the homeland of the Tatar people. From Tartary, the vast landmass extending from north of Japan all the way to the east of Iran, the Tatars had joined the armies of Genghis Khan back in the thirteenth century. Since the 1300s, many had settled in and around Kazan, building the largest and most important city of Tatarstan. This prosperous trade town, at the confluence of the Kazanka and Volga rivers, lies some 750 kilometers east of the Russian capital, Moscow.

Mukhlisa's last name, Bubi, comes from the name of the Tatar village of Ij-Bubi or Izh-Bobino, about 320 kilometers from Kazan. Her father was a *mulla*, a Muslim priest, and served as the village imam, or preacher, leading congregational prayers, officiating at weddings, supervising funerals, and sometimes adjudicating minor disputes, for example over inheritance. Mukhlisa absorbed the basics of Islamic learning at home. She learned to recite and memorize passages from the Quran on her mother's lap and she pored over manuscripts in her father's little library.

Mukhlisa's mother and grandmother were both respected *abistay*s, literate women who taught local girls. Children, girls as well as boys, learned to read and write and acquire basic familiarity with arithmetic, along with lessons in piety and propriety. Tatar *abistay*s shaped a big part of Tatar religious life, educating girls, counseling women and preaching to women's gatherings. On occasion, the *abistay*'s home provided a setting for women to mingle, to exchange poems, chant hymns, discuss family-related matters, seek legal advice or embark on copying manuscripts together.

In 1887, when Mukhlisa reached the age of eighteen, she was on her way to becoming an *abistay* herself. Her parents married her off to a *mulla*, but the marriage proved unhappy, and a combination of historical forces, personal preferences and sheer chance propelled her in a different direction. As a young Muslim woman, she joined the so-called Jadid movement. The word *jadid* means "new" and in nineteenth-century Tatarstan it carried connotations of being modern, progressive and civilized. The Jadid movement presented its ethos as rooted in the best of traditional values and oriented toward an even better future. Like other advocates of this movement, Mukhlisa wished to improve the status of Russia among the civilized nations of the world, and to elevate the status of Muslim subjects within the Russian Empire.

Muslims had been part of Russia ever since the Tsars extended and consolidated their power base beyond Moscow. As early as 1552, Ivan IV (r. 1547–1584), known as the Terrible, had conquered Kazan. Living up to his name, he had slaughtered half the population. Those who survived defied forcible conversion to Russian Orthodox Christianity. For generations, they glorified Suyum Bike, the city's last Muslim queen, who had honorably fought the Tsar. During Mukhlisa's lifetime, invoking the beloved queen's name still stirred solidarity among Tatar Muslims, especially the Jadids.

It was only in the eighteenth century that Empress Catherine II (r. 1762–1796) finally abandoned the policy of converting Muslims to Christianity. Instead, she allowed the creation of an organized hierarchy for Islam in parallel with that of Russia's Orthodox Church. As a gesture of goodwill toward her Muslim subjects, in 1787 she started having typeset editions of the Quran printed for the first time. Moreover, she sanctioned Islamic law, or sharia, as a framework for adjudication among Muslims. Soon the "Spiritual Administration of Muslims" was established. The identification of religion with the "spiritual" was most significant. This organization gathered and kept records on the Muslim population and supervised mosques, always with an eye to enforcing loyalty to the empire. The court appointed a high-ranking *mulla* to administer Muslim affairs. Charged with issuing sharia-based rulings, called *fetvas*, this *mulla* served as the empire's *mufti*, or jurist. Overseeing the operation of a network of judicial courts through a hierarchy of sharia judges, or *qazyis*, the *mufti* regulated such matters as Muslim marriage and divorce and the division of inheritance.

By the late 1850s, Tsar Alexander II (r. 1855–1881), Catherine's great-grandson, had launched the Great Reforms, to the benefit of his subjects. Most notably, the abolition of serfdom across the empire freed millions of peasants from bondage to landowners. The intellectual horizon brimmed with a sense of optimism that progress was not only desirable, but also possible and close at hand. Eventually, the reformist agenda manifested itself in a succession of social movements and revolutionary uprisings in Russia. The most important of these was the world-changing Russian Revolution of 1917.

Among Tatar communities, too, the Great Reforms inspired the Jadids. They called for social reform and advancement through the renewal of Islamic teachings. The Tatar Jadids adhered to the ideology of progress, as did many of their contemporary Muslims in India, Iran, Turkey and Egypt. Combining a variety of political and religious ideals to revive and renew Islamic teachings, the Jadids produced newspapers, pamphlets and other publications. Their mantra was education, education, education.

By the 1890s, Jadid ideals had blossomed in Kazan and reached even the backwaters of the Volga-Urals. Mukhlisa's brothers were both Jadids in Ij-Bubi. She too found herself inspired by the Jadids' educational innovation and their emphasis on women's education. At the time, Mukhlisa had left her unhappy marriage and moved back with her parents. With unwavering encouragement from her mother, father and brothers, she opened the first modern-style school for girls in Tatarstan in 1897. The curriculum integrated Russian, European and Islamic elements in thought and practice. Besides general literacy, young girls received instruction in hygiene, home crafts and household management skills. Coursework included geography and arithmetic, as well as Quran recitation and calligraphy in Arabic script.

The Ij-Bubi school for girls issued certificates that qualified graduates for employment as teachers elsewhere. Mukhlisa's name and the reputation of her school drew students from Kazan and as far away as Moscow, Samarkand, Bishkek and even

Siberia. Many of the school's graduates became educators. Demand for qualified teachers was on the rise as girls' schools proliferated across Russia.

A collection of letters from a student in Mukhlisa's school gives us a sense of her loving devotion to preparing a new generation of enlightened women, who went on to lead fruitful lives and steered their families and communities towards a better future. The writer, Rayhana, came from a wealthy merchant family in the province of Nizhny Novgorod in central Russia. Having developed a close relationship with her school principal, she wrote:

> You cared for us day and night, molding us into good human beings, showing us more kindness than our mothers and fathers, providing us with advice and counsel to bring us happiness. As grateful as I am, I know that I cannot even return one tenth of what you gave us.

Rayhana seems to have been a somewhat rebellious girl, and in 1908 her parents had sent her to attend Mukhlisa's school, eight hundred kilometers from home, to learn some discipline. Here is some advice that her mother gave her:

> In the same way you care that your clothes be beautiful and clean, never forget to adorn yourself with knowledge and good manners. A human becomes a human not with clothes but with knowledge and good manners.

After four years at the school, Rayhana returned home to teach girls at a new school that a wealthy woman had funded in her home town.

Russian officials questioned the political motivation behind the educational and intellectual activities of the Jadids. To them, the Jadids' loyalties seemed divided – and too close to the Ottoman capital, Istanbul. At the time, the Ottomans still rivaled the Tsars politically and militarily. Some feared that the Jadids functioned as an arm of the Ottoman Empire. Indeed, some members of the Jadid movement did openly praise the Sultan's pan-Islamism, a vision of uniting all Muslims under a single leader. For that, the Jadids paid a price. Russian police eventually shut down Mukhlisa's school in 1911, calling it a hotbed of radical intrigue. Several of the teachers and staff were arrested, including Mukhlisa's brothers.

Undeterred, Mukhlisa pursued her calling as a pedagogue elsewhere. She accepted the invitation of a wealthy Muslim family from Troitsk, a day's ride from Moscow, to head a new school that they had funded and named after Suyem Bika, the sixteenth-century Tatar queen. In her speech at the opening ceremony of the school in the academic year 1914–1915, Mukhlisa emphasized the necessity of women's education for progress and articulated her ideas about the role of Islam in education:

> The crucial factor in the happiness and preservation of our nation and the most necessary thing for strengthening our religion is educating our women and adorning them with knowledge.

Amid the turmoil of the First World War, Russia underwent waves of political upheaval that eventually climaxed in 1917. In February of that year the last Tsar abdicated and entrusted imperial rule to a provisional government, which in turn was to govern through a hierarchy of local community assemblies, or *soviets*. Eight months later, in October, armed rebels dissolved the provisional government and transferred all power to the soviets. In time this arrangement consolidated as the gargantuan Union of Soviet Socialist Republics.

Also in February, Russian women acquired the right to vote as citizens equal to men. This was one year before some women were given the right to vote in Britain and two years before the ratification of the 19th amendment to the US Constitution granted this right to American women. With the decisive support of several sharia judges, Muslim women in Russia embraced not only the right to vote but also the mandate to join political organizations and convene congresses as they desired.

On April 23, 1917, Muslim women from different regions of Russia congregated in Kazan. Mukhlisa and the other participants at the All-Russian Muslim Women's Congress proposed reforms to women's social status, called for the enhancement of women's marital rights, and discussed the implications of equality between men and women. As voting citizens of Russia, some of the participants inclined more toward socialism or even communism than did others. Still, they all agreed to propose ways and means within the framework of sharia. After intensive debates, the group submitted its resolutions to the All-Russian Muslim Congress. Held in Moscow between May 1 and May 11, 1917, this second gathering brought together approximately nine hundred Muslim delegates, more than a hundred of them women.

A sensitive topic that had lingered from the women's congress in April was the demand to ban polygyny or polygamy – the practice of a husband taking more than one wife. The matter was revisited in Moscow but remained unresolved. Since sharia underwrote this practice, approaching it called for caution. While some based the demand for equality on the Quran, others insisted that unqualified equality between men and women in all aspects of social and political life contradicted sharia.

Still, the Moscow Congress arrived at a significant resolution concerning the administration of Muslim affairs. The Muslim Spiritual Assembly was to be restructured on the revolutionary model of distributing authority through consultative assemblies or soviets. It was to be renamed the Spiritual Administration of Muslims. Moving forward, the *mufti* and the collegiate body of the sharia-based judges who worked with him ought to be elected, not appointed from above. As representatives of Muslim constituents, the *mufti* and the *qazyis* were required to hold regular meetings to hear, discuss and decide on requests from their constituents. The most surprising outcome of the Congress in Moscow was the unprecedented election of a woman as a *qazyi* or sharia judge to serve on that body. This revolutionary endorsement of women's equality with men marked a unique development not only among Russian Muslims but also in the history of the Muslim world. Of the three women nominated for the post, Mukhlisa Bubi won.

Two months after being elected, Mukhlisa resigned her post at the school in Troitsk and started working as a sharia judge. She took on the robe of religious authority with determination and hope, despite critics who opposed her election as "a religious and political mistake," probably citing the hadith that states "Succumbing to women's authority augurs doom." For the next twenty years of her life, Mukhlisa directed the Department of Family Affairs that dealt with issues of divorce, dowry, marital consent, inheritance and other legal complaints from women. Her work as a *qazyi* complemented her accomplishment as an educator. She brought the same commitment to adjudicating family disputes in the Muslim community that she had displayed in running schools for girls. As a sharia judge she took it upon herself to instruct *mulla*s and imams who served under her jurisdiction to protect women's rights, especially to desist from performing second marriages for already married men.

Besides serving as a sharia judge, Mukhlisa continued to publish her own articles on women's legal rights. In an August 1917 newspaper article, she noted the abundance of complaints she received about cases of polygyny. Stating that no one had the right to force a woman into becoming a married man's second, third, or fourth wife, she also condemned *mulla*s who officiated at such marriages.

Under Mukhlisa's supervision, the Spiritual Administration of Muslims officially instructed *mulla*s on how to officiate at marriages. She drafted a model marriage contract that defined and defended women's nuptial rights within the framework of sharia, requiring officiants to spell out the conditions and exceptions of the deed in loud and clear terms. A woman ought to be advised of the terms at the time of matrimony, noting that she could reserve the right to initiate divorce proceedings directly and independently should her husband marry a second wife without the first wife's agreement, get drunk or gamble often, contract venereal disease, prove to be impotent, or fall short of providing for the household.

Perhaps there was a personal side to Mukhlisa's passion here. Her own marriage had foundered early on but, keeping up appearances for her parents' sake, she had stayed with her husband for years. When she decided to leave in 1897, her husband refused to grant her a divorce for twenty years. Whatever personal motivations she may have had, Mukhlisa's reputation spread as a firm but fair *qazyi*. She handled family cases from all over Russia.

Besides complaints about men marrying more than one wife, Mukhlisa adjudicated cases of divorce, inheritance, and child custody, among others. Islamic law allows for women to inherit from their parents, husbands, siblings, and children. So disputes over property rights could, and sometimes did, get quite complicated.

Even though the October revolution of 1917 eventually turned against Islam in Russia, early on it had little impact on Mukhlisa's work as a sharia judge. In the beginning, the Communist revolution upheld its promise of emancipating and empowering minorities; its leader, Lenin (1870–1924), even called on Muslim Russians to be the world's vanguard in the struggle against Western colonialism. Meanwhile, the Muslims were divided. The Communist Party had a few Muslim members, most of them former Jadids, who founded such organizations as the Muslim Socialist Committee. Meanwhile, Mukhlisa continued to push for women's rights as her sacred duty. The communist government welcomed her efforts to end such practices as child marriage and also levirate marriage (when a widowed woman had to marry a male relative of her deceased husband).

As in other moments in her life and career, Mukhlisa sought to balance tact with tenacity. For example, she took action in the aftermath of the Povolzhye famine that raged in the Volga area. The catastrophe had left an estimated five million dead in just a few years, between 1920 and 1922. She did her best to support the survivors, signing her name to a letter published in *Pravda*, the Communist Party newspaper, urging Muslims around the world to come to the rescue of the victims. She drafted and ratified a sharia-based ruling to allow women to obtain a divorce and the right to remarry by pleading that their husbands had vanished because of the famine. At the same time Mukhlisa continued to reach out to ordinary Muslims, reminding them of the importance of an Islamic upbringing for the new generation.

Stressing that "our mothers and grandmothers preserved our sacred religion of Islam facing many obstacles in teaching and learning religion," she lamented that opportunities to learn at the feet of women teachers, or *abistay*s, had all but disappeared. She urged men, particularly local imams, to encourage women and children to attend mosques and listen to sermons, especially in the evenings and for Friday congregational prayers. She highlighted the religious merit in training girls as the primary conveyors of religious knowledge and ethics to the next generation: "Teaching Islam will be a duty that they will face in the future."

Given the full-blown anti-religious campaign of the time, and its repression of Islam, such pronouncements were brave. State propaganda targeted Islam through a number of periodicals. Professing loyalty to Islam became hazardous.

The dreaded Joseph Stalin (1878–1953), who succeeded Lenin as the General Secretary of the Communist Party of the Soviet Union's Central Committee, increased the pressure on Muslim religious institutions. Just months after he took office in 1922, the

People's Commissariat for Education forbad religious study in Muslim schools. Party institutions vilified Islam as reactionary and "the most bourgeois of all cultures in the Soviet Union." Within a few years, the number of active Muslim sites of religious gathering, mosques and Sufi centers dwindled from tens of thousands to a few dozen. The sharia courts were dissolved and Mukhlisa's role as a *qazyi* came to an end.

Targeting Tatarstan as the core of the revolution's Islamic problem, the Communist Party launched a process of de-Islamicization there. The policy demanded that Tatar writings should henceforth appear only in the Cyrillic script. The ban on the Arabic script was a bid to sever the Tatars' centuries-long link to the Islamic past and to the contemporary Muslim world. Even harsher persecutions followed. Thousands of mosques, schools and charities were forced to shut down. Muslims had to "voluntarily" hand over their premises to be turned into Soviet "cultural and educational centers." Falsely accused of collaborating with alien anti-revolutionary forces, the populations of entire villages faced deportation and displacement. Countless *mulla*s and imams were arrested, imprisoned and exiled to labor camps or *gulag*s. Attempts at eliminating Islam from public life climaxed in 1937 when Stalin's security police, the NKVD, terminated Muslim autonomy in the USSR.

Mukhlisa also became a victim of the NKVD in 1937. In November of that year she was arrested on suspicion of being a member of a counter-revolutionary bourgeois-nationalist organization, and of serving as a liaison between that organization and foreign intelligence services. The case was entirely fabricated but Mukhlisa was executed a month later. Along with millions of others, she had been declared an anti-revolutionary by Stalin.

What could Russian Muslims have contributed to Islamic history had the communist revolutionaries not destroyed them? Outside Russia, decades passed before other countries followed their example of promoting the rights of women: Indonesia in

1964, Iran in the 1970s, the Palestinian territories in 2009, and Malaysia in 2010. How many hopes were dashed by Mukhlisa's disappearance from the court?

Since the collapse of the USSR, Mukhlisa Bubi has enjoyed a heroic resurrection. She is remembered and revered as an educator, judge, and leader. In 2014, the Tatar Museum of Islamic Culture in Kazan opened a permanent exhibition devoted to her life. The city's theater staged a play about her. There are plans to launch a special prize in her honor. Many Tatar Muslim women today aspire to claim some part of her legacy.

# 17

# Halidé Edip
## (ca. 1884–1964)

## AUTHOR OF THE NEW TURKEY

Nationalism is a potent ideology that has played a significant role in the history of Islam in modern times. This
can be clearly seen in the life and career of the Turkish
Halidé Edip Adivar (ca. 1884–1964). Writer, activist, soldier and
politician, in the early twentieth century she was both an agent
and observer of the historical transition from the Ottoman Empire
to the Turkish Republic.

Born into a privileged family in Istanbul, Halidé enjoyed the best
kind of late Ottoman upbringing. Sadly her young mother died
when Halidé was an infant but her father, Mehmet Edip, placed her
under the loving care of her maternal grandparents. From the many
women of the household she learned Turkish folktales and customs,
and, besides reading, writing and basic arithmetic, she learned to
recite and memorize passages from the Quran. In her memoirs, she
credits her grandmother with molding her religious outlook.

Halidé was eleven when her father remarried and took her
back into his home. Mehmet Edip served in the newly built Yildiz
(Star) Palace as a secretary and treasurer to Sultan-caliph Abdul-
Hamid II (r. 1876–1909). This position enabled Edip to employ
an English governess and excellent tutors for his daughter.

Secondary schools for girls, known as *inas ruşdiє*s, had opened as early as 1859, but many families in Istanbul preferred not to send their puberty-age daughters to schools with male teachers. In 1870 the number of students in secondary schools for girls was around two hundred in a city of well over half a million people. Halidé's father, however, felt that times were changing and enrolled his eleven-year-old daughter at the American Girls College. The American Board of Commissioners for Foreign Missions had founded the school in 1876 on the Anatolian shore of the Bosphorus. There Halidé received an exacting education from the faculty, most of them women. In 1901 she became the first Muslim to graduate from the school, with an age-appropriate education in literature and other liberal arts, including a good grasp of English and French. Her familiarity with foreign languages served her well throughout her life.

Upon graduation, the seventeen-year-old Halidé got married for the first time. Her husband, twenty years her senior, had tutored her in math. Over nine years of marriage, the couple had two sons together. Meanwhile, Halidé continued to read and extend her education as best she could.

Looking to its European peers, mainly France, the Ottoman Empire invested in the signifiers of the modern age. By the middle of the nineteenth century, it had railways, censuses, telegraphs, steam ships, world fairs, clock towers and buildings in European styles. The thousands of photographs taken by Abdul-Hamid II feature educational facilities and students, military personnel and facilities, technologically advanced life-saving and firefighting brigades, factories, mines, harbors, hospitals and government buildings.[1] Proponents of Ottoman modernity celebrated the "synthesis of these European elements with Muslim Ottoman Civilization" as an answer to the question, "How to become modern while remaining oneself?"[2]

Newspapers, pamphlets and periodicals gave voice to a women's movement that developed in Ottoman countries, centered on

Istanbul. Columnists and other public intellectuals wrote on women's proper dress and manners and encouraged education and political activity. Halidé followed the conversation closely.

Demands to improve women's education and encourage their participation in civic life resonated with the reformist concerns of thousands of Ottoman civil servants, army officers, intellectuals and activists. They called themselves the Young Turks. Resolved to remedy and reverse what they saw as the decline of the Ottoman Empire, the Young Turks combined reformist and revolutionary elements in their agenda. First and foremost, they wanted to limit the Sultan's exercise of power, moving away from autocracy to constitutional government. The country's constitution of 1876 had already framed the debate a generation earlier.

The Young Turks contended that belonging to the Muslim community (*ummet*) under the authority of the Ottoman Sultan-caliph failed to sustain the unity of the empire. They proposed Turkishness as the new foundation of national unity. Instead of loyalty to the throne and the profession of Islam, the Young Turks stressed Turkishness in lineage, language and mentality. They promised to elevate the Turkish nation to the station it deserved among the modern nations of the world.

In the wake of the Young Turk Revolution in 1908, Halidé focused on the intersection of nationalism and the women's movement, and took on both causes. She wrote newspaper columns on the issues of the day. In her first novel, published when she was twenty-four, she introduced forward-looking heroines into modern Turkish literature. In line with the priorities of the Young Turks, she addressed questions such as "Who is a Turk?" and "What is Turkish?"

Halidé considered that Turkish women were the core of the Turkish family, which in turn formed the heart of the Turkish nation. Her literary output of a dozen or so novels and many short stories exemplifies the meeting-point of literature and nationalism.

The Young Turks made primary school education mandatory for girls. Halidé joined forces with a leading female educator, Nakiye Elgün (1882–1965), to overhaul the curriculum and staffing policies at the Women Teachers' Training College in Istanbul.

Women were encouraged to participate in lectures, performances and exhibitions at the New Turks' social and cultural club, called the "Turkish Hearth," *Turk Ocagi*. Halidé often lectured there, wrote for its widely distributed periodical, *Turkish Homeland*, and served on the executive committee.

Thanks to recent political reforms, women had acquired the right to initiate divorce more easily, although polygamy continued to remain legal for men. Halidé left her first husband in 1910, when he told her he wanted to take a second wife. Living in a bigamous marriage ran contrary to Halidé's vision of the family as the harmonious microcosm of an integrated nation.

Meanwhile, like other proponents of nationalism before and since, the Young Turks had contradictions to resolve. For generations the Ottoman Empire had included, and to varying degrees integrated, several other identity groups besides the Turks. A new notion of "pure" Turkishness led the New Turks to idealize the ancient culture of faraway Turkistan and Tataristan, even as they centered their activities in Anatolia. This nascent nationalism left little room for non-Turks.

In the years following the 1908 revolution, Greeks, Macedonians, Bulgarians, Kurds and, most famously, Armenians paid dearly. Over a million Armenians and Greeks disappeared from Ottoman lands, and most of them from the face of the earth. Under the provisions of the Treaty of Lausanne, almost 900,000 Greek Orthodox Christians from Ottoman territories were exchanged for some 400,000 Muslims from Greece.

As early as 1912, the start of the Balkan Wars signaled that keeping the Ottoman Empire united had become more difficult than ever. The wars redrew the boundaries of several new

European countries that seceded from the empire, and the First World War continued the process.

During World War I, Halidé served as a ranked member of the national resistance army. She married a physician and fellow nationalist named Adnan in 1917. Later, when the Turkish Republic made having surnames a necessity, Dr. Adnan took the last name Adivar, which means "renowned." In 1918 the Ottoman Empire collapsed. When the war ended in the fall of that year, after the Armistice of Mudros (October 30), a defeated Turkey was about to be occupied by the French, Italians, British and Greek Allied forces. Italian troops occupied Antalya; the Greeks landed in Izmir on May 15, 1919 and advanced toward the interior. As one of their first actions, the occupying forces dissolved the parliament in Istanbul. Sporadic resistance and guerrilla warfare started in Anatolia.

On May 23, 1919 Halidé Edip addressed a rally of thousands at the Sultanahmet Square, near Istanbul's Old Bazaar. She urged them to fight against the occupation forces. Her bust stands there today in memory of that occasion. Immediately after delivering her speech Halidé traveled to Anatolia to participate in the Turkish Independence War (1919–1922). She joined the "inner circle" of the leader of the resistance movement in Anatolia, Mustafa Kemal Pasha, better known by his later title, Ataturk – Father of the Turkish nation. He had been active during the Young Turk Revolution of 1908. Drawing on her language skills, she read and reported on the foreign press, collected news and wrote for the Anatolian Agency, and translated and drafted English and French correspondence. On occasion, she served as a liaison with American and British officials in Istanbul.

In all of this, she faced great danger. Both the occupying foreign forces and the Ottoman Sultan wanted to see the nationalists disappear. British forces deported fifty-five of them to Malta. Doing his part, the *seyhulislam*, the highest religious authority of the Ottoman Empire, issued a *fetva* against the nationalists, decreeing that any Muslim believer had the duty to kill the rebels. Mustafa Kemal, Halidé, her husband and a handful of other prominent nationalist figures were the prime targets. Halidé and her husband went into hiding in Üsküdar, near the American Girls College. The nationalists and those religious groups that supported them countered with a *fetva* of their own, which identified the government as traitors. Meanwhile, Turkish nationalist armies made inroads into central Anatolia under the future Ataturk and his comrades in arms. Joining them, Halidé conducted relief work under the banner of the Red Crescent. She spent the better part of 1922 with the army and was promoted in military rank. Soon the nationalists prevailed, and the Grand National Assembly abolished the Sultanate. Ataturk declared the establishment of the Turkish Republic in 1923 and himself assumed the role of its first president. Moving the capital from Istanbul to Ankara, he appointed Halidé's husband to his cabinet. On March 1, 1923 Ataturk officially abolished the caliphate and ordered all members of the Ottoman dynasty to leave the country.

After years of warfare Turkey was impoverished and in ruins. The population had declined by 20 percent. Over three million Ottoman subjects had lost their lives. Famine and cholera and typhoid epidemics swept the land.

Ataturk stressed Turkism as the cornerstone of the nascent Turkish Republic. He sought to break with the Arab influences in the Ottoman Empire by launching radical reforms in language policy and the writing of history. He changed the Turkish alphabet, using roman instead of Arabic letters. He set up a new and distinctly European dress code and put forward a manifesto of cultural mobilization in service of the new state. He effected the secularization of the family code and the enfranchisement of women as he liquidated the religious institutions of the Ottoman Empire.

Halidé had helped to bring down the *ancien régime* and was instrumental in shaping its alternative, the Turkish Republic.

While she agreed with Ataturk's broad vision of the new Turkey, she also had some qualms about it. She, too, regarded the nation as the natural social and political unit, but unlike Ataturk, she drew on references to Islamic teachings to make her point. She placed the family at the center of the nation and women at the center of the family. She wrote:

> It was the mother who started agriculture and industry in their most primitive aspects, in order to feed and to clothe her young. She also created the family as the unit of human society. The rest evolved around that. Since nature appointed mother to create the family, and since aggregations of families have inevitably grown into nations. Nature also endowed woman with two seemingly incompatible characteristics, extreme conservatism and extreme revolutionism, customs, traditions, language. Thought and literature evolve and accumulate around the family or group of families.[3]

Once the Armenian and Greek communities had vanished, Turkey's religious makeup shifted from about 80 percent Muslim before World War I to 98 percent after the war. Even as Turkey became increasingly homogenous, Ataturk's efforts to heighten "Turkish" national consciousness came at the expense of a more encompassing Islamic identity. He considered Islam one of the main obstacles to the westernization and modernization of Turkey.

Halidé took a more moderate approach: she upheld the Quran as a source of enduring truths and made reference to it in defending women's rights. For example, when it came to promoting equal pay for women, she quoted the Quranic line, "Men shall have the benefit of what they earn and women shall have the benefit of what they earn."[4] She wrote:

The supreme aim of Islam being social justice, it could not leave half of society out of consideration . . . Islam's greatest significance for the modern world is that it is the first system which accords property and economic rights to women and makes them independent of the guardianship of their men.[5]

She defended the *sharaf* (Islamic veil) as a symbol of social integration. To her, wearing a veil expressed, simultaneously, the Islamic faith of the people and nationalist sentiments. She wrote:

The Koran (Sura 24, verse 31) commands women to pay due regard to their dress, enjoining them to wear veils that will cover the sides of their head, their bosom and their ornaments; there is no order to cover their faces, still less are they expected to shut themselves up and abstain from social activities. The Prophet's own wife was one of the most remarkable women, with a great social reputation. In this commandment we see two things, first, that women should be decently dressed, even if they desire to make themselves beautiful, and secondly, what is more significant, they are asked not to use their beauty and sex to exploit their fellow-creatures. This is just what a modern feminist or any healthy society aims at.[6]

Halidé's husband and a few other like-minded intellectuals founded an opposition party in 1924. Hardly a year passed before the government ordered it shut down, claiming it had instigated a religious insurgence and a plot to assassinate Ataturk. Erring on the side of caution, Halidé and her husband left Turkey in 1926.

The couple spent well over a decade in Europe, the United States and India. Their time away coincided with Turkey's cultural revolution under Ataturk. Dr. Adnan was tried in his absence but completely exonerated. A year later Halidé paid a brief visit to Istanbul.

During her time in Europe and the United States, Halidé Edip was politically silent but intellectually productive. Over the course of four years in England (1924–1928) she wrote her memoirs and several novels, which were serialized in the Turkish dailies. In 1929–1939 she lived mainly in Paris, where her husband was a lecturer in Turkish at the École des Langues Orientales Vivantes. In 1929 she visited the United States, where she went on a lecture tour of various American universities. In the 1931–1932 academic year she lectured at Barnard College, the girls' school of Columbia University in the city of New York. In 1935 she traveled to India to lecture in universities in Delhi and other cities. There she had a chance to meet the outstanding nationalist leaders of the subcontinent, most notably Mahatma Gandhi. She wrote that India "felt to be nearer to my soul-climate than any other country not my own."[7] Back in Paris, she wrote more novels, including her only novel in English, *The Clown and His Daughter*.

Halidé and her husband returned to Turkey for good on March 5, 1939. Four months had passed since Ataturk, their comrade in arms and the father of the Turkish republic, had died on November 10, 1938. Within months, Halidé was appointed head of the newly founded Department of English Language and Literature at the University of Istanbul. Over the following decade she trained a generation of young students with whom she worked on new translations of Shakespeare's *Hamlet* (1941), *As You Like It* (1943), *Antony and Cleopatra* (1943) and *Coriolanus* (1945). She also translated George Orwell's *Animal Farm* (1952).

She assumed dynamic roles in educational, national and women's projects, actively participating in politics. After serving as the Izmir deputy in the Turkish Parliament from 1950–1954 she retired from political life in January 1954. Soon after her husband of thirty-eight years died in July 1955, Halidé's health deteriorated. She died at home on January 9, 1964.

Halidé Edip Adivar's ideological fluidity subtly changes our understanding of nationalism, gender relations, and identity politics in Turkey at a painful time of transition. Even as a multi-ethnic religious empire was becoming a secular nation-state, Halidé wrote as an Ottoman, a Young Turk, a Muslim, a woman and an intellectual. She created a point of intersection between competing ideologies such as modernity, Islamism and westerni-zation. Halidé Edip Adivar remains one of the most-read Turkish writers of her generation.

# 18

# Noor Inayat Khan
## (1914–1944)

## THE ANXIETY OF BELONGING

A s a Muslim-born woman of mixed Indian and American parentage, who was born in Russia, grew up in England, came of age in France, and died in Germany, Noor Inayat Khan (1914–1944) navigated cross-cutting identities long before "identity politics" became fashionable. She is best known for her courageous actions as an Allied spy during World War II.

Noor's parents had met in San Francisco. Visiting the United States from India in 1911, her father, Inayat Khan (1882–1927), headed a group of Sufi musicians performing at the city's Columbia Theater. Before World War I, the European and American avant-garde had taken a shine to the exotic Oriental arts, including painting, music and dance. Inayat Khan and his fellow musicians belonged to the Chishti Sufi Order, a large religious organization that for centuries had promoted devotional music, as a way of experiencing the divine presence. Inayat Khan came from a good Muslim family that included a long line of musicians trained in the North Indian style of classical music. He sang both folk melodies and classical ragas, and played the veena, a large stringed instrument. Ora Ray Baker (1892–1949), a Christian-born woman in the audience at one of his performances, found herself drawn to the musician in a shimmering shirt, with his dignified beard, intense black eyes, shoulder-length wavy hair and, most of all, his immeasurable charisma. Facing family resistance to her marrying "a brown foreigner," Ora and Inayat eloped to London and were married there. A shared spiritual quest took the newlyweds to St. Petersburg and Moscow, where their first child was born on January 1, 1914. They named her Noorunnissa, "Light of Women," a title carried three centuries earlier by the Mughal queen Nur Jahan. To friends and others, Noorunnissa was Noor, but at home they endearingly called her Babuli, daddy's little girl.

The unexpected outbreak of World War I in the summer of 1914 compelled the family to leave Russia. At the time, India was a British colony, so a subject of the crown and his American wife could settle in England with ease. The Khans set up home in London, renting a place in the elite Bloomsbury district. Three more children came, two sons, Vilayat and Hidayat, and another daughter, Khayrunnissa. Several luminaries of the time called that neighborhood home, among them the economist John Maynard Keynes (1883–1946), the writer Virginia Woolf (1882–1941), and other members of the famous Bloomsbury group. Although Noor's family lived a stone's throw away from them, they inhabited an entirely different world.

Noor and her siblings were too young to comprehend why, but their father found post-war London overbearing. The British government kept a suspicious eye on its Arab, African and Indian subjects, not least on those who had come to live in Britain. Tensions increased in April 1919, when a massacre took place in the north Indian city of Amritsar, with British troops killing hundreds, possibly more than a thousand, unarmed Muslim, Sikh and Hindu men, women and children, and wounding several thousand more. It was a watershed moment for the leaders of the Indian Independence Movement, most notably Mahatma Gandhi (1869–1948). On a visit to London, Gandhi is said to have extended a personal invitation to Inayat Khan to join the movement. Khan declined. The nature and extent of Inayat Khan's political involvement remains unclear, but he sympathized with the movement. It remains unclear whether he helped raise funds to support it. However, a brief association with a questionable charity named Anjuman Islam brought him to the attention of the British police. With encouragement from his family, and a growing circle of admirers drawn by his Sufi practice and teachings, he resolved to pursue his calling in France.

In or around 1920, Noor's family crossed the Channel, seeking a more welcoming environment. In the post-war years many European intellectuals were searching for meaning and a new direction in their beliefs. Some of them called attention to the mystical teachings of the Sufi Islam and Hindu traditions. With such voices in the background, Inayat Khan founded the Sufi Order of the West. Like many Sufi orders in India, going back to the time of Queen Nur Jahan's father-in-law, the Mughal emperor Akbar (r. 1556–1605), Inayat fused elements of Islamic and Hindu traditions. He readily embraced all spiritual seekers – not only Muslims, Christians and Jews, but also Hindus, Buddhists, Jains, Sikhs, Gnostics and others – as wayfarers on the same divinely illumined path. Initiates in his Sufi order, called *mureeds*, or disciples, sought to attune the fast tempo of modern life to the timeless wisdom of the mystics. They called Inayat Khan Hazrat – "His Eminence," or "The Revered."

Hazrat Inayat Khan's family settled in Suresnes, a suburb of Paris, where a disciple had bequeathed him a large house, which he called Fazal Manzil, "The Abode of Blessing." Noor and her younger siblings grew up in the Abode of Blessing. Her father's disciples came to pay homage, not only from France but also from Holland, Germany and Switzerland. Basking in the presence of spiritually aware parents, the Khan children listened to their mother tell stories and recite poems, some of which she had composed herself. The children knew her as Amma; their father and his disciples called her Ameena Begum, "The Faithful Lady."

At home, the Khans spoke English mixed with Inayat Khan's mother tongue Gujarati. The principal language at the Abode of Blessing was music. Hazrat Inayat Khan shaped and conveyed his spiritual message by singing and playing songs and melodies. Abba, as his children called him, taught Noor and her brothers to savor musical harmony as a manifestation of the divine; as a road map for self-discovery and self-expression; as a way of attuning oneself to the beauty, balance and truth of God's creation. Abba's music and his message suffused Noor's life.

Hazrat Inayat Khan exercised much influence over the lives of those around him, not least Noor, his loving daughter and devoted disciple. His death at age forty-five left a gaping void. He had gone away for a few months to visit his native India for the first time in almost two decades and unexpectedly died there. Ameena Begum collapsed in grief and the thirteen-year-old Noor had to shoulder more responsibilities for the household.

A few months later, in May and June 1927, Noor and her brothers traveled to their father's ancestral home with their mother. Ameena Begum hoped to salvage her children's inheritance, but there were difficulties, the trip was cut short, and Noor's arranged marriage, which her father may have planned, fell through.

A significant highlight of Noor's journey to India was a pilgrimage to the town of Ajmer and the tomb-shrine, or *dargah*, of Moinuddin Chishti (ca. 1141–1236). He was an important figure in the Chishti Sufi order to which her father had belonged and through which he had met his own teacher. Ever since Chishti's time, Indian Sufism had embraced and emphasized the ethos of serving God's created beings, irrespective of status, creed or color, as the principal path to spiritual ascent. Formal dogma and ritual ranked as inferior means of drawing close to the divine when compared to dedicating oneself to serving all humans. To this day, hundreds of thousands, perhaps millions, of pilgrims, Muslims and non-Muslims alike, come to Chishti's *dargah* to pay homage. As they give alms to the poor or share in a meal together, they remember the great Sufi known as the Gharib-newaz—the Succorer of Strangers. Back in the day, the redoubtable King Akbar had displayed his veneration for Moinuddin by making as many as fourteen pilgrimages to Ajmer during his reign.

Noor had internalized the Sufi ethos of service. As a young adult she took on the responsibility of running the Abode of Blessing. She looked after her siblings and took care of their increasingly frail mother. Meanwhile, she attended high school at the Lycée de Jeunes Filles in Saint-Cloud, a half-hour walk from home. She displayed a knack for learning languages, German and Spanish besides French and English. Noor liked literature, and wrote poetry. Here are a few lines addressed to her mother:

> Beloved! Ah! Beloved Amma,
> A treasure stored deep in our heart,
> 'Tis flowers of our gratitude,
> Behold! For their petals are carved
> With Allah's own heavenly art.[1]

In 1931 Noor started her studies at the École Normale de Musique in Paris, playing instruments, singing and learning musical theory. She already played the veena, the harp and the piano at home, and formal training allowed her to expand her repertoire and to polish her skills. A year later she enrolled in child psychology classes at the Sorbonne University. She made good progress in both fields. Although visitors to the Abode of Blessing often saw her as a quiet, even reclusive, young woman, Noor gradually grew more expressive in style and manners – what one might call her Paris *chic*.

Unlike most Sufi orders in and outside India, the Sufi Order of the West cultivated mysticism and stressed spirituality in everyday life over asceticism. The Abode of Blessing housed valuable artworks, especially original paintings. Wearing fine clothes and traveling in style mattered to Noor's family. In the summer of 1933 she and her brother Vilayat took a trip to the fashionable south of France, and later toured Spain, Italy and Switzerland together. As a young woman, Noor visited the Hague, giving recitals and piano lessons at the invitation of one of her uncles and two of her late father's disciples. Within her family, marrying well was important, so a serious friendship with a classmate in Paris who, although an initiate in the Sufi Order of the West, was only a Jewish immigrant from Turkey, was discouraged by her relatives.

Noor continued to compose poems and write stories for children. In 1938, she contributed to the children's page of the Sunday issue of France's oldest newspaper, *Le Figaro*. In response to good reviews of her work, the *Children's Hour* on Radio Paris featured some of her whimsical tales. Before passing her twenty-fifth birthday, Noor published her English translation of selected Buddhist fables, *Twenty Jataka Tales*, with accompanying illustrations made by a Sufi Dutch aristocrat and friend of the family. She contemplated publishing a children's newspaper. But then the world and her life changed.

When World War II began, Noor and her younger sister volunteered for the Union des Femmes de France, or the French Red Cross. More than half the population of Paris left the city; Noor, too, left for England, accompanied by one of her brothers and their mother. Her other brother joined the French Resistance. Within six weeks of their departure, in the spring of 1940, the French army surrendered, leaving Paris a battleground between Nazi occupiers and the Resistance.

Nazi racism ran in the face of the principles of universal oneness and harmony that Noor's father had instilled in her. Longing to serve a greater cause, she dedicated herself to the war effort in England. She joined the Women's Auxiliary Air Force (WAAF) in November 1940 and for several months trained as a radio operator and telegraphist, learning Morse code and technical skills. Noor's enlistment records show her name as Nora and her religion as Church of England, Christian.[2] Was this a clerical oversight? According to her biographer, Shrabani Basu, "Noor did not want to appear exotic . . . She never spoke to her colleagues about her father, or her ancestry, or the Sufi faith . . . Noor had to reinvent herself."[3] But she remained close to her siblings and devoted to her mother.

Under severe pressure, Britain's wartime prime minister, Winston Churchill (1874–1965), toiled to counter German offensives by any means. In July 1940, barely a month after the fall of Paris, he oversaw the launching of the Special Operations Executive (SOE), a secret organization with the express mission "to set Europe ablaze," carrying out sabotage and cooperating with anti-Nazi resistance groups.

Noor came to the attention of the SOE. Her skills as a radio operator, coupled with what were noted as her "interesting linguistic qualifications which might make her of value for operational purposes,"[4] outweighed any suspicions about inherited sympathies for the Indian Independence Movement. She officially started special SOE training in February 1943. As described by a co-trainee, "She was very quiet, very shy, and often wore a nervous smile." She spoke English with a tinge of an accent difficult to identify. Within weeks, the newly arrived young woman with brown hair, hazel eyes, and a high, sweet but faint voice vanished from the premises of SOE.

On the night of June 16, a single-engine Lizzie plane dropped Noor on French soil. Her secret assignment was to establish a radio link between a local Resistance network in Paris and the British War Office. Posing as a nanny, she showed up daily for clandestine work on a university campus in the south west suburbs of Paris, just north of Versailles. She transmitted critical information, signing her messages as Madeleine, the name of a character in one of her children's stories.

Scarcely a week after Noor's arrival, the Gestapo struck, taking down the network she worked with in one swoop. The leader of the network, six radio operators under his command, and scores of other Resistance members disappeared within days of June 24. Madeleine/Noor fled. She was now the only undercover radio operator for the Resistance in Paris.

She survived for 119 days, three times longer than the average SOE and French Resistance radio operator. Despite the danger, she kept the wire open to England, sending the names of captured agents, scheduling weapons drops and coordinating the escape of downed pilots. Meanwhile, Nazi secret police and military intelligence units, the Gestapo and Abwehr, acquired her codename and general description. They looked out for her everywhere. On foot or riding her bicycle around Paris neighborhoods, Noor took great care in carrying out her mission. Each time, she had to set up the radio, string out the long antenna wire, transmit messages and then pack up before being noticed by a surveillance vehicle or one of many local informants. All of this in under twenty minutes. She went about her clandestine activities under a disguise that came easy, as a chic Parisian woman.

She once made her way to Suresnes, her old neighborhood, where she hoped to find someone she could trust. This was a dangerous decision, but she went to seek help from a former neighbor. It pained her to see foreigners occupying her childhood home, the Abode of Blessing. Eventually, not the neighbor but the young sister of a fellow member of the Resistance betrayed Noor. Nazi agents stormed her apartment and took her on October 13, 1943.

Soldiers dragged Noor into German counter-intelligence headquarters at no. 84 Avenue Foch, where she underwent days of interrogation, then weeks of torture. Failing to break her, the captors sent her to Germany on November 26, 1943. After several months in Pforzheim, sixty miles from the French border, they transferred her, in shackles, to the Dachau concentration camp.

There, thousands of Jews, dissidents, members of the Resistance, and others awaited what the Third Reich had euphemistically termed *Nacht und Nebel* – night and fog. Noor Inayat Khan faced the firing squad on September 13, 1944, four months shy of her thirty-first birthday.

Noor posthumously received Britain's George Cross, a high civilian decoration awarded for acts of the greatest heroism and most conspicuous courage in circumstances of extreme danger. Her 1949 citation reads:

> She refused to abandon what had become the principal and most dangerous post in France, although given the opportunity to return to England, because she did not wish to leave her French comrades without communications.

The French awarded Noor the Croix de Guerre, a military decoration, and named a square in Suresnes as Cours Madeleine. Every year on July 14, Bastille Day, a band plays in her honor outside the Abode of Blessing, her erstwhile home. Plaques in her memory hang in the agricultural school in Grignon, where she started sending Resistance radio messages, and in Dachau, where she died. Since 2012, a bust of her looks out from Gordon Square in London, not far from where she once ran around as a child and, later, sometimes sat on a bench with a book on her lap. In 2018 a campaign began to have her portrait featured on a British banknote.

Noor's life-story resonates with the concerns and sensitivities of our times, when millions of Muslims and others continue to negotiate their place in "the West," newcomers as well as those with deep roots. Today, the nearly three million Muslims in the United Kingdom, the four million in North America, and the forty million in Europe and Oceania must also navigate difficult waters.

# 19

# Umm Kulthum
## (ca. 1904–1975)

## LODESTAR OF UNION

The Six-Day War in 1967 between Arab and Israeli armies reshaped the Middle East. It left 20,000 men dead or wounded, most of them Egyptians. The Egyptian singer Umm Kulthum (ca. 1904–1975) brought calm, comfort and courage to her people at that moment of collective shock, grief and despair.

On the morning of June 5, 1967, Israeli bombers strafed airfields in Egypt, Syria, Jordan and Iraq. By June 10, Israeli troops had seized land from four Arab countries: the West Bank and Jerusalem from Jordan, the Golan Heights from Syria, the Sinai Peninsula and the Gaza Strip from Egypt, and Saudi Arabia's Tiran Island in the Red Sea. The combined area of the newly occupied territories was three times larger than the original area envisaged for a Jewish state. The scale and speed of the change had no precedent in the two decades since the formation of the state of Israel in 1948 had sparked the Arab-Israeli conflict. The loss of human life, honor and territory left many inconsolable, not merely in Egypt and the Arab nations directly involved but among Muslims worldwide.

Long before the onset of the Six-Day War, Umm Kulthum had been Egypt's sweetheart. Her voice and songs had formed part of the backdrop of Egyptian life for decades. After 1967 she became an international icon.

Umm Kulthum was born in a poor village 120 kilometers north of Cairo. Some date her birth to 1898 and others to 1904, because official birth certificates were not issued consistently in Egypt at that time, especially not in rural areas. Her father, Ibrahim, worked the land. Fellow villagers respected him as a pious, hardworking man and sometimes asked him to lead daily prayers as their imam. Like many peasants, Ibrahim took on other jobs. He recited poems and sang songs at weddings and religious gatherings, especially on the day of celebrating Prophet Muhammad's birth and on the two *eid*s – Muslim feasts at the end of the month of Ramadan and the end of the Pilgrimage season. This often took him away from his village to visit towns and villages along the eastern Delta, traveling mostly on foot or by third-class train. Often Ibrahim took his little girl Umm Kulthum with him to sing dressed as a boy.

After the end of World War I, Cairo quickly became the largest Arab city. It absorbed waves of peasant migrants who came in search of a better life, including Umm Kulthum's family when she was almost twenty. They all came for jobs, for money, and for all the other opportunities that the city had to offer. The Egyptian capital was also the cultural capital of the Arabic-speaking world. The city's bustling theater district housed European-style cafes, restaurants, open-air music halls and an opera house. Wealthy families invited artists to perform in their mansions in the Garden City neighborhood on the eastern banks of the Nile in south Cairo.

Umm Kulthum found opportunities to sing at wealthy women's gatherings. Her sonorous voice, clear diction and ability to convey deep meaning, together with the wide repertoire of religious and other popular songs she had mastered, kept her in demand. One thing leading to another, she found a patron and the patron found a phonograph; soon, with her father's approval, the young singer entered the lucrative world of commercial music. By 1928 she was a star. Her artistic authority grew during the 1930s and 1940s. Over the course of her career she made three hundred recordings and appeared in six movies.

In 1952, Egypt took on the political leadership of the Arab world. Under the command of the charismatic Gamal Abdel Nasser (1918–1970), the Young Officers Revolution ushered in a new era of vigorous optimism. Sharing the public's enthusiasm for creating a better Egypt, Umm Kulthum offered her talents to the revolution, performing patriotic anthems and singing songs to elevate the nation's spirit. Nasser dubbed her the voice of Egypt.

Britain, France and, to some degree, the United States eyed Nasser's rise to popularity with concern. Against the backdrop of the Cold War, with tensions escalating between the West and the Communist Bloc, they felt they had to do something. First, they thought it necessary to curb the enthusiasm felt for General Nasser across the Arab world and beyond. Forming a coalition, Britain, France and Israel invaded Egypt in 1956. To display his commitment to placing Egypt's interests first, Nasser declared that the Suez Canal belonged to the Egyptians, thereby rejecting the historical claims that the French and the British had made to the canal that connected the Mediterranean Sea to the Red Sea. His popularity skyrocketed, and he proceeded with greater confidence. He took socialist measures, pushed for modernizing reforms and called on all Arab countries to unite under the banner of Pan-Arabism and Arab nationalism. As his admirers gained power in several Arab countries, Nasser forged an alliance with the Arab Socialist Ba'ath Party and the Syrian Communist Party, a union that culminated in the formation of the United Arab Republic, bringing Egypt and Syria together as one nation under a single flag. The role of Arab nationalism in shaping Islamic history during the second half of the twentieth century can scarcely be exaggerated.

At the peak of Arab nationalist fervor, Umm Kulthum projected Arab dignity and authenticity. Her masterful singing of classical Arabic verse, her vocal stamina and impeccable diction remained unmatched. Moreover, she endeared herself to the younger generation by singing lyrics composed by that the younger intellectual poets of the day. Acknowledging Umm Kulthum as a cultural icon of Pan-Arabism, Nasser adopted one of her songs as the national anthem of the United Arab Republic:

> By God, it has been a while
> For our troops to advance like thunder
> Promising never to return,
> Except with a roaring victory.
>
> O! glory our glory,
> You who was built by us,
> By toil and pain,
> Never to go to waste.
>
> Who shall protect Free Egypt?
> We shall protect her with our weapons.
> Land of the Revolution, who will sacrifice for her sake?
> We will, with our souls.
>
> The people advance like the light,
> The people stand like mountains and seas,
> Volcanoes of anger, volcanoes erupting,
> Earthquakes digging the enemy into their graves.[1]

Then came the Six-Day War in 1967. Israel had resolved to crush the spirit of revolutionary Arab nationalism. After Egypt's humiliating defeat, Nasser launched a media campaign to rekindle that spirit, drawing on his country's dominant position in the recording, radio and film industries. The widespread distribution of Egyptian cultural products throughout the Arab Middle East and North Africa became a matter of nationalist policy and national urgency.

Umm Kulthum now had a new role to fulfill in the national arena. The 63-year-old diva renewed people's hope as she gave concert after concert and organized and participated in fundraisers. The intensity, diversity and sincerity of her activities outstripped those of other celebrities. When most artists made token donations of twenty Egyptian liras at a time, she gave twenty-thousand liras. She never held back. Within weeks after the Six-Day War ended, she had recorded a repertoire of patriotic songs to raise public morale. She spoke at a national assembly of women and her insistence led to the formation of the National Assembly of Egyptian Women. This worked as an umbrella organization to address the pressing economic and emotional needs of families.[2] From August 1967 she began to take her concerts beyond Cairo, so that people in smaller cities and villages could see and hear her. Performing outdoors in stadiums, pavilions and under large open-air tents, she drew as many as 12,000 people to each concert. Men, women and children came to listen and participate in a national ritual of solidarity. Many donated personal items of monetary and sentimental value – wedding rings, trinkets, jewelry and gold ingots. Once, a child brought a handful of dirt, and it was auctioned for three-thousand liras, roughly equivalent to seven-thousand dollars.

Umm Kulthum also toured the world, drawing attention to the plight of her nation and donating the proceeds to help the victims of the Six-Day War. Her performance at the Olympia Theatre in Paris was dubbed by the French press as "an Arab political-artistic rally." She drew not only the Arab diaspora community, but also Europeans. A man in Paris told her that she made him feel united with his Arab brothers, Palestinians in particular. She went on to give concerts in Morocco, Kuwait, Tunisia and Lebanon, all in less than six months. Radio broadcasts carried her concerts across national boundaries in the

Middle East, North Africa and beyond. Back in Egypt, newspapers reported how she had spent the *eid* with a needy family and celebrated the Prophet's birth alongside Tunisia's queen. She was an ambassador at large. Unable to hold back his tears, a listener in Tunisia said that "Her romantic words remind me of the tragedy of our homeland with colonialism and my tragedy with colonialism." She kept saying:

> I am a patriotic woman and I love my country. I am ready to make any sacrifice for the sake of the freedom of my country – the concern of all Egyptians.

Here are a few lines from one of her most renowned songs, "Atlal":

> Give me my freedom, release my hands
> Indeed, I've given you yours and did not try to retain
>   anything
> Ah, your chains have bloodied my wrists
> I haven't kept them nor have they spared me
> Why do I keep promises that you do not honor?

Umm Kulthum wished to "say to each European face to face that every centime, pence or cent they give to Israel is transformed into a bullet killing an Arab person."

She sang, and people sang with her all over the world. Even those who could barely understand the meaning of her words responded to her performances with emotion, regardless of where they lived or where she sang. Her voice forged solidarity. Setting lyrics by poets from Lebanon, Sudan and the United Arab Emirates – even Omar Khayyam's words, translated from Persian into Arabic – she evoked and emphasized the idea of Arab cultural unity. Through her songs, she connected the Kuwaiti traffic policeman with the Algerian immigrant in Paris, the Jordanian Bedouin with the Libyan Sufi, and all of them with the Egyptian people. The Sudanese greeted her as the "Uniter of the Arabs" whose voice was a weapon.

Nasser's government backed Umm Kulthum at home and abroad, investing in her accomplishments as a "public relations" campaign for the cause of Pan-Arabism and Arab nationalism. The state capitalized on her concerts as a means of showing that Egypt did not stand alone in facing the impact of the Six-Day War. The Arab world needed to stand united and prepare for a prolonged war. As the proclaimed "Artist of the People in the Battle,"[3] Umm Kulthum received a state award and even a diplomatic passport. Her trips resembled state visits. In turn, she contributed the equivalent of $2 million to the rebuilding of Egypt's armed forces, and countered the psychological damage inflicted by the war.

Critics wondered why a celebrity of her caliber never spoke truth to power at home. She never seems to have encouraged her audiences in Egypt to challenge the existing military, political and social systems that ruled them. Some radical critics of the government protested that her "intoxicating" performances diverted the public's attention away from pressing social and political problems at home.

Umm Kulthum continued her tours, visiting Sudan, Libya and Jordan. Later, reflecting on her fundraising trips, she said, "They were intended to clearly encourage co-operation among all Arabs and to convert it into something tangible. I wanted to prove that we (Arabs) are together in the view of Israel and that we (Arabs) are together in facing military aggression." Performing in the Libyan cities of Tripoli and Benghazi in 1969, the proceeds of ticket sales went to the Palestinian Liberation Organization (PLO): she raised a total of £150,000 ($345,000). The walls around her carried posters that said, "Peaceful solutions will only continue over our dead bodies." Even the title of one of her new songs spoke volumes: "The Tempest" was also the name of the militant wing of the PLO. Indeed, she stated that "committed Arab art is one of the weapons of the revolution," and that "in the blaze of the armed Palestinian revolution a new Arab people is born." Giving voice to Arab sentiments at the time, she openly spoke about the liberation of occupied lands, mentioning Palestine in particular, and characterized the freedom fighters' work as "the model path for the restoration of Arab Palestine."

During her tour of Tunisia, Umm Kulthum prayed in the historical al-Zaytunah mosque wearing a *burnus*, a traditional long, hooded cloak. The appearance of the visit matched its timing in importance. On the first anniversary of the outbreak of the Six-Day War, the first lady of Tunisia had joined the iconic artist in reciting the Quran, singing religious songs and praying, in remembrance of those killed a year earlier.

Umm Kulthum's political and artistic legacy go hand in hand. When she died in 1975, an estimated four million mourners came to her funeral, walking her body to its burial place. When asked about her place in Egyptian society, a man on the streets of Cairo exclaimed,

"Umm Kulthum? She's like the pyramids of course!"[4]

# 20

## Zaha Hadid

### (1950–2016)

### CURVES IN GLASS AND CONCRETE

In an interview with the *Guardian*, the renowned architect Zaha Hadid (1950–2016) complained, "You cannot believe the enormous resistance I've faced just for being an Arab, and a woman on top of that. It is like a double-edged sword. The moment my woman-ness is accepted, the Arab-ness seems to become a problem."[1]

In her enviably creative and enormously productive life, Zaha Hadid redefined architecture for the twenty-first century. Her accomplishments draw attention to the rising visibility of women's achievements in recent decades. Deftly handling the double-edged sword of gender and identity to her advantage, the Iraqi-born naturalized British citizen tore down obstacles and won almost every prestigious award in architecture. She literally laid her mark on the skylines of major cities around the globe, from London to Shanghai, from Baku to Vienna, and from Seoul to New York.

Born on October 31, 1950 in Baghdad, Zaha Hadid exemplifies the social drive and stellar accomplishments of a pioneering generation of migrant Muslims in Europe and North America. Her father, Muhammad Hadid, had named her Zaha, which means "flamboyant" and "showy." This was neither a classical nor a common name for girls in Arabic. She lived up to the potential of her name, in fact, she transcended it.

As a young man, Muhammad Hadid (1907–1999) discovered himself in Mosul, an important Iraqi town on the west bank of the Tigris River, four hundred kilometers north of Baghdad. He wished to be rich and powerful. The surname he chose for himself, Hadid, and the first name he later gave his eldest son, Foulad, both mean "steel" or "iron," conveying a sense of his solid determination to succeed. Marrying Wajiha al-Sabuni, daughter of a wealthy and influential family in Mosul, helped him achieve both goals.

With the defeat of the Ottoman Empire in World War I, in 1918 British forces occupied the former Ottoman Province of Iraq and some territory beyond it, including Mosul. As they did with Palestine, the British brought Iraq under mandate, meaning that they claimed the right to rule the land without taking possession of it. Mosul had abundant oilfields and for Britain to keep its rivals, especially Turkey, away from them proved an urgent matter. However, massive protests broke out against non-Muslim suzerainty. As a compromise, the British Crown granted sovereignty over Iraq to a close Muslim ally, the Hashemite royal family. Named after Hashem, an ancestor of the Prophet Muhammad, the Hashemites were respected as *sharif*s or descendants of the Prophet through his daughter Fatima and her eldest son, Hasan. For centuries, the family had served as stewards of the holy cities of Mecca and Medina. The leader of the Hashemite clan, Emir Hussein, son of Ali (ca. 1853–1931), had spearheaded the revolt against the Ottomans in 1916. Rejecting the platform of the Young Turks, who were gaining in power at the expense of the Sultan-caliph, he had relied on the British promise of support for Arab independence. The British later helped Emir Hussein's grandson, King Faisal of Iraq (r. 1921–1933), to the throne in Mandatory Iraq, which became known as the Kingdom of Iraq under British Administration.

Long before Zaha's birth, her father had moved the family to Baghdad. Thanks to Wajiha al-Sabuni's family connections, as well as his own initiative and resolve, Muhammad Hadid drew close to the inner circles of power there. At the age of twenty-five he helped start Iraq's National Democratic Party, bringing together a group of left-leaning liberal young men. When King Faisal declared the end of the British Mandate in 1932 and claimed independent sovereignty, such men came to play ever more significant roles in building Iraq as a modern nation-state. As a political leader, Muhammad Hadid rose through the ranks of the finance ministry, served as an elected member of the Iraqi parliament representing Mosul and held other high-ranking bureaucratic positions.

British armies reoccupied Iraq during World War II, using the country's facilities without restriction, but effectively leaving the Iraqi government to function semi-autonomously. So Baghdad remained a small but thriving city, with about half a million inhabitants, sharply divided along class lines. The Hadid family belonged to the upper class and Zaha inhabited a world very much apart from most Iraqis but surrounded by the leading members of the Iraqi National Democratic Party. As she later reminisced, "The ideas of change, liberation, freedom and social reform were so important to me."[2] She discovered a love for architecture bubbling inside her at the age of six. As she later recalled, seeing the drawings and models of a house that her aunt planned to build in Mosul, "triggered something."[3]

Zaha was scarcely eight years old when crisis hit. The Hashemite Kingdom of Iraq collapsed in 1958. The gap between the haves and the have-nots had toppled the ruling dynasty. Nationalist army officers under the leadership of Brigadier Abd-Al-Karim Qasim (1914–1963) seized power in what became known as the July 14 Revolution. The mob stormed the royal palace, massacred the royal family, and paraded mutilated bodies on the streets of Baghdad. The military government abolished the monarchy and declared Iraq a republic. Numerous families associated with the monarchy left the country, some moving to nearby

Jordan, where a cousin and close companion of their murdered king held the Hashemite throne. Even though Zaha's father had strong ties to the monarchy, his party had joined a coalition with the opposition, including the Ba'ath Party that upheld the Pan-Arabist vision of the Egyptian leader Gamal Abdel Nasser. Muhammad Hadid served as the one and only non-uniformed member in the new military cabinet. Like many of the wealthy landowners and professional classes, Zaha's family remained prominent after the revolution.

Five years later, another coup or revolution occurred in Iraq. In the heat of the Cold War, the tension between the West and the Communist Bloc, this second revolution steered the nation leftward and brought Iraq into the Soviet sphere of influence. The new government was no longer friendly towards Zaha's family. Their wealth was nationalized, a euphemism for confiscation by the state. Zaha's father sent her abroad. For a while, she attended boarding schools in England. In 1972, she graduated from the American University of Beirut with a bachelor's degree. This institution of higher learning has played an instrumental role in the modern history of Islam.

Before the onset of the devastatingly long Lebanese Civil War in 1975, Beirut had the nickname Paris of the East. Many upper-class Iraqi families visited often. Like Paris, albeit on a different scale, Beirut offered culture, education, books, banking. Despite almost five decades of internecine war and instability, Beirut is still a nerve center of Arab life. The American University of Beirut, originally founded as the Syrian Protestant College in 1866, still stands. Back in 1871, its president, an American missionary, proclaimed: "This college is for all conditions and classes of men without regard to color, nationality, race or religion. A man, white, black, or yellow, Christian, Jew, Mohammedan or heathen, may enter and enjoy all the advantages of this institution for three, four or eight years."[4] In 1920, the college acquired its current name, and over the course of more than a century and a half, it has trained tens of thousands of doctors, engineers, nurses, teachers and graduates in business-related fields.

With a degree from the most reputable Arab university, Zaha Hadid moved back to London, gaining admission to the prestigious Architectural Association School. There she studied under leading architects of the day, receiving her Diploma Prize in 1977. For her fourth-year student project, she had designed a hotel in the form of a bridge, expressing ideas that continued to inspire her work over the following three decades. One of her teachers described her as "the inventor of the 89 degrees. Nothing was ever at 90 degrees."[5] At graduation, Rem Koolhaas (b. 1944), called her "a planet in her own orbit,"[6] and another master architect, Elia Zenghelis (b. 1937), remembered her as his most outstanding pupil.

After graduation, Zaha was apprenticed at the Office for Metropolitan Architecture, in Rotterdam, the Netherlands, working for two of her former professors. Then in 1980 she opened her own architectural firm. Her brother had married into the Moroccan royal house,[7] and backed by her own ties to Arab elites, Zaha's prospects were promising – but the journey was not always smooth.

Early on, Zaha's designs largely remained unbuilt. Already in her early drawings, from the 1970s, she insisted on putting a slant on things. Nothing was ever simple or straight in her designs. Spectacular and innovative as they were, implementing them would be costly. So she drew more immediate fulfillment from lecturing architecture students. First teaching at her own college in London, over the years she went on to lecture on architecture at some of the world's finest academic institutions: Cambridge, Vienna, the Hochschule für bildende Künste in Hamburg, Harvard, Chicago, Ohio State, Yale and Columbia University in New York.

The field of architecture is fiercely competitive as its players vie to have their work showcased in coveted venues, win prizes and receive recognition from exclusive groups of patrons and critics. Receiving the Gold Medal for architectural design in 1982 gave Zaha Hadid a good start. Then in 1988 the Museum of Modern Art (MOMA) in New York showcased her work and her fame skyrocketed. After that she won almost every possible award. Most notably, in 2004 she won the Pritzker Architecture Prize, the most prestigious award in architecture, considered on a par with the Nobel Prize. She was the first woman to receive this prize and, in the words of the head of the deciding jury, Lord Rothschild: "Her energy and ideas show even greater promise for the future."[8] She also won the Stirling Prize, the United Kingdom's most prestigious architectural award. Later, she became the first and only woman to receive the Royal Gold Medal from the Royal Institute of British Architects. The American Academy of Arts and Letters named her an honorary member and the American Institute of Architects, an honorary fellow. The United Nations Educational, Scientific, and Cultural Organization (UNESCO) recognized her as an "Artist for Peace," and the Republic of France honored her as a Commandeur de l'Ordre des Arts et des Lettres. In 2012 Queen Elizabeth II made her a Dame Commander of the Order of the British Empire.

Zaha Hadid had plenty of confidence, for good reason. She was not keen to be characterized as a woman architect, or an Arab architect. She was simply an architect.[9] She knew that excellence depends on cooperation. So she worked with the very best associates she could find. In her own words:

Sometimes, women feel they have to do everything – work, manage the house, look after the children – but there's too much to do. So you have to learn early on that you can't do everything yourself, and you have to learn to trust other people to work on your vision. Teamwork is very important to me, and that's why things are manageable. I can't take credit for my projects alone – many people in my office have contributed to them.[10]

As with the works of many leading creative minds, Hadid's do not sit easily in a single category. Not that this has stopped critics from employing such opaque labels as abstractionism,[11] deconstructivism[12] and parametricism in the course of their analyses. Certainly, Hadid envisioned ways to shape glass, steel and concrete as few others could, resulting in buildings that seem to challenge the laws of physics. The London Aquatics Centre, built for the 2012 Olympics, and the Guangzhou Opera House in China both possess a fluidity that almost has the observer believe they are in a state of perpetual motion. Hadid herself, who often used dense architectural jargon, could also describe the essence of her style very simply: "The idea is not to have any 90-degree angles. In the beginning, there was the diagonal. The diagonal comes from the idea of the explosion which 're-forms' the space. This was an important discovery."[13]

Zaha Hadid died of a heart attack on March 31, 2016, in Miami, Florida. Nobody expected this. Several of her buildings remained under construction at the time of her death. She was buried in England, between the tombs of her father Mohammad and brother Foulath. In her will she left £67 million between her business partner and members of her extended family. Her architectural legacy visibly reflects her innovative spirit.

Zaha Hadid did not emphasize being Muslim. Still, that does not diminish the significance of her role in drawing attention to the status and aspirations of Muslim women in the twenty-first century.

# 21

# Maryam Mirzakhani

## (1977–2017)

## THE PRINCESS OF MATHEMATICS

Nationalism takes many shapes and forms in different times and places, as we have seen from Halidé Edip's literary articulations of Turkishness, Noor Inayat Khan's selfless sacrifice, and Umm Kulthum's musical expression of pan-Arab ideals. During the closing decades of the twentieth century, a stark combination of nationalism and religious revivalism appeared. Notably in Iran, the heirs of the nineteenth-century Osuli *ulama* took the reins of the most rapidly modernizing nation in the Middle East, with a booming oil-based economy. The results are still unfolding and, so far, the record is riddled with contradictions. Aspects of the unlikely transformation in women's education can be seen in the short life but exceptionally brilliant achievements of Maryam Mirzakhani (1977–2017).

At eighteen, she solved a mathematics problem that had puzzled experts for twenty-four years. She won a ten-dollar cash prize for that from her professor. Nineteen years later, at the age of thirty-seven, in 2014, this Iranian-American mathematician received a Fields Medal, the highest recognition of mathematical excellence worldwide. She was the first woman to do so and to this day remains the only woman among sixty medalists in over eighty years.

The historical contribution of women to mathematics is scarcely acknowledged. Eric Temple Bell's popular book on renowned mathematicians, entitled *The Men of Mathematics*, includes only one woman. And her name is misspelled. First published in 1937, Bell's book justly celebrates the leading nine-teenth-century mathematician Carl Friedrich Gauss (1777–1855) as the Prince of Mathematicians. As one of the greatest mathematicians of the early twenty-first century, Maryam Mirzakhani deserves public recognition as the Princess of Mathematics, symbolically and substantively.

Born on May 12, 1977 in Tehran, Maryam grew up in a middle-class Muslim family with her father, an engineer, her mother, a homemaker, and three siblings. She was almost two when her native country underwent a revolution. Known as the Islamic Revolution of 1979, this major turning point abolished the ancient institution of monarchy in the land and culminated in the establishment of the Islamic Republic of Iran. It also marked a high point in the ongoing process of Islamic awakening that had gained momentum worldwide in the heat of the ongoing Cold War.

During the 1970s, Iran was a rapidly westernizing country, the closest ally of the United States in the Persian Gulf region and a byword for urban growth, industrial development and modernization. Enriched and emboldened by the inflow of petrodollars, foreign currency gained from selling crude oil on the international markets, the country's ruler Mohammad-Reza Shah Pahlavi (1919–1980) took it upon himself to lead the world's only Shia-Muslim nation state to what he envisaged as "the gates of great civilization." Domestic detractors and foreign critics objected to the man himself and his plans, eagerly pointing out elements of inconsistency in both. Convinced that he had a divine calling to push forward, the Shah saw no contradiction between being modern and being Muslim. His tragic flaw, which brought about his downfall, was that he failed to tolerate dissent. Dissidents came from many backgrounds, from mild liberals to staunch communists, from merchants and government employees to the Shia *ulama*. Ayatollah Khomeini (ca. 1902–1989) who belonged to the upper ranks of the Shia *ulama* and had a history of criticizing the Shah, took the lead in giving voice to public protests. Eventually and unexpectedly, he toppled the royal throne.

Running the country proved more difficult than staging a revolution and ousting the Shah. Problems appeared the day after the declared victory of the Islamic Revolution on February 12, 1979. The newborn Islamic Republic found itself overstretched in all directions. Then, on the last day of summer in 1980, Iraqi airplanes bombarded Tehran's airport, launching the twentieth century's longest war of attrition in the Middle East. Between 1980 and 1988, hundreds of thousands of Iranian and Iraqi citizens were killed, maimed or otherwise harmed. Meanwhile, the Islamic Republic had to combat domestic armed rebellion, resist international sanctions and provide basic services for the country's population. The record of achievement left much to be desired.

During the difficult years of the Iran–Iraq War (1980–1988) Maryam's parents protected their children. As Maryam recalled in a 2008 interview, "It was important for them that we have meaningful and satisfying professions, but they didn't care as much about success and achievement."[1] She finished elementary school the same year that the Iran–Iraq War ended.

In the post-war years, officially dubbed the Era of Reconstruction, improving the educational system constituted a top priority. Making the Islamic Republic an exemplar of success depended on having a robust system of education. Maryam had the good fortune of benefiting from top-level educational policies. Had she been born a decade earlier, many of those opportunities would never have been available to her. The so-called Cultural Revolution had dashed the opportunities of thousands of deserving students.

The Constitution of the Islamic Republic mandates free elementary and high school education for all citizens of Iran.[2] During the 1980s the government strictly banned private schools, considering them a blatant example of the discriminatory ways of the old order that the revolution had promised to reverse. However, the quality of public education could vary drastically, from place to place, even from neighborhood to neighborhood. In order to provide the very best education for the nation's brightest students, the government resolved to create schools that catered for those with superior aptitude in math and science. In 1988, along with a hundred or so other eleven-year-old girls, Maryam Mirzakhani scored high in a competitive examination and got into Farzanegan, Tehran's exclusive school for gifted female students.

A lifelong friend she made on their first day at Farzanegan, who shared a bench for the next seven years, recalls that "math was the only subject in which Maryam was not among the top students in the sixth grade."[3] Once, when she received a score of sixteen out of twenty, equivalent to a B, she tore up her test results, saying that she had had it with math! Commenting on the incident of the exam years later, Maryam remembered that she hardly fancied herself a theoretical mathematician. She had a personal understanding of why "many students don't give mathematics a real chance . . . [because] without being excited [about it] mathematics can look pointless and cold."[4] Instead, as a young girl she reveled in reading novels and had a passion for writing. Along with her friend, she would wander round the bookstores close to the school and would buy and read anything she could find.

It took an inspiring older brother and several great teachers to get her seriously interested in mathematics and coach her on the path to becoming one of the best theoretical mathematicians of her age. Soon Maryam and her best friend were spending hour after hour thinking and talking about mathematical problems.

Educators often make a difference. A capable woman with a vision of excellence for her school, Farzanegan's principal ran a tight ship, recruiting a team of star teachers and fostering a competitive but enriching environment for the students. She worked hard to guarantee that students at Farzanegan had the same opportunities as the students at the best schools for boys. Thanks to her commitment and hard work, she convinced the officials at the Ministry of Education to allow female high schoolers to participate in preparatory summer math/science camps away from home and to let girls compete in competitions abroad.

Extracurricular activities played a big role in developing an interest in mathematics among high school students. Summer camps run by instructors at Sharif University in Tehran and the intensive training marathon of the International Math Olympiad competitions thrilled Maryam and her teammates. A workshop on graph theory, a college-level course that she attended in the summer after her ninth grade (1993), had a major impact on Maryam's growing interest in math and resulted in her first publication in a peer-reviewed journal, at the age of sixteen. Maryam participated in the Math Olympiad competitions in the eleventh grade (1994), and she and her long-standing school-friend were the first two female students on the national team. That year in Hong Kong and the following year in Canada, Maryam achieved gold medals, in one case with a perfect score, and attained the Olympiad's highest honors.

With such stellar accomplishments behind her, Maryam had no difficulty getting into Sharif University of Technology. Applicants had to outperform the competition in the *concours*, a breathtaking series of examinations in all subjects on the high school curriculum. Acceptance rates in Sharif and other top-tier universities remained below 5 percent of applicants, though Olympiad students were readily accepted without having to undergo the *concours*. Maryam entered Sharif University in 1995 and graduated in 1999. More than a decade after the launching of the Cultural Revolution, Iranian universities had revived. In fact, the 1990s witnessed an unprecedented growth in the number of universities and university students nationwide. For the first time in Iranian history, the number of female university students equaled and soon surpassed that of male students. At Sharif, Maryam had a chance to meet the best and brightest of her generation, including inspiring professors and fellow students. She proved her mettle again during her freshman year by winning a token prize for solving a hard problem that the world-renowned Hungarian mathematician Paul Erdős (1916–1996) had formulated two-and-a-half decades earlier. Her professors treated her like gold. The more time she spent on mathematics, the more fascinated she became. A less pleasant experience in her junior year, in March 1998, was being a bus crash in the early hours of the morning, when the vehicle went over a cliff, killing seven of the best students of her year.

Maryam Rezakhani started graduate school at Harvard University. She later characterized her initial state of mind there as "clueless."[5] To keep pace, she sometimes jotted down notes in her native Persian language. However, from the beginning, she distinguished herself with a strong will to learn and her rigorous mind. Within five years, in 2004, she obtained her PhD.

From Cambridge, Massachusetts, Mirzakhani flew across the Atlantic to Oxford, where the newly established Clay Mathematics Institute found her research in line with its mission to further the beauty, power and universality of mathematical thought in human progress, culture and intellectual life. Concluding her fellowship there, she returned to the north east United States, starting her first faculty position at Princeton University. In a room in the mathematics department she made her own, she covered the blackboards in equations, sharing with faculty members and students the many ideas she wanted to explore further. Soon Stanford University got ahead of Princeton, offering Maryam a full professorship at the age of thirty-two. Based at Stanford, she went on to win multiple prestigious awards. The crowning achievement was the Fields Medal, in recognition of "her outstanding contributions to the dynamics and geometry of Riemann surfaces and their moduli spaces."[6] The journal *Nature* listed her among "10 People Who Matter" in 2014.

The advanced mathematical concepts and methods that Maryam Mirzakhani employed remain indecipherable to lay people. As she put it, "The beauty of mathematics only shows itself to more patient followers."[7] Nevertheless, her contemplative depth comes through in her confession that "I am a slow thinker and have to spend a lot of time before I can clean up my ideas and make progress."[8] She declared:

I don't have any particular recipe [for developing new proofs] . . . It is like being lost in a jungle and trying to use all the knowledge that you can gather to come up with some new tricks, and with some luck, you might find a way out.[9]

She characterized the moment of discovery, the feeling of being on top of a hill and having a clear view, as the most rewarding part of this imaginative wandering in the forest. In her own words, "Of course, the most rewarding part is the 'Aha' moment, the excitement of discovery and enjoyment of understanding something new. But most of the time, doing mathematics for me is like being on a long hike with no trail and no end in sight!"[10]

Great a mathematician as Maryam Mirzakhani was, her lifestory comprised more than just a narrative arc dotted with successive professional achievements. She must have radiated a sense of perspective and focus; she seems to have persevered[11] and never settled for half measures; and she must have had a tenacity always to do better, tirelessly revising and polishing her work. She refused to go for the easy low-hanging fruit, and her advice was, "Know what you want, and don't get distracted."[12] People who knew her well also highlighted her modesty, curiosity, dedication to excellence and above all her humanity.

Many professional mathematicians reminisced in the *Newsletter of the American Mathematical Society* that they saw more in Maryam Mirzakhani than a "genius." Rather than being eccentric, which is the prototypical portrayal of "genius" in the entertainment industry, her friends remembered that "she had the same qualms and worries as the rest of us," adding that "she was a lovely person. We loved her for who she was, and we would have loved her just the same even without her honors and awards."

The American mathematician Alex Eskin (b. 1965) remembers her as "the nicest and most positive person I have ever met."[13] Cumrun Vafa, an Iranian-American professor at Harvard, remembers her helping disabled students navigate the campus.[14]

Maryam was intensely private and never promoted herself. Reportedly, her parents heard she had received the Fields Medal through the media. She explained later that she did not think it was such a big deal! With a gracious smile, she stepped aside from the spotlight. At the peak of her productivity as a mathematician in 2008, she confessed, "I prefer solo activities; I enjoy reading and exercising in my free time."[15] Together with her husband, a Czech-born colleague named Jan Vondrák, she raised their daughter, Anahita, pursued mathematics, and enjoyed listening to audio books, among other things.

Maryam was diagnosed with breast cancer in the spring of 2013. Her treatments were difficult and painful but within four years the cancer had spread, first to her liver, then to her bone marrow. Two months and two days after her fortieth birthday, she died, much too soon.

The shockwaves of Maryam Mirzakhani's untimely death went beyond the circle of mathematicians. In her native Iran she was given a farewell worthy of a national heroine. Her face appeared on the front page of newspapers nationwide. Her tragic death as a young mother raised public awareness of several issues. Learning that Maryam's efforts at obtaining citizenship for her daughter had failed, sixty members of the Islamic Consultative Assembly (the Iranian legislative parliament) proposed a law that would automatically grant Iranian citizenship to children of Iranian mothers married to foreign men. Despite nationwide sympathy for the star mathematician and her daughter, the proposition fell through. Thousands of children born to Iranian women who have married foreigners, especially refugee men from Afghanistan in Iran, remain in limbo. The initiative continues.

Maryam Mirzakhani's work had a profound influence on many young mathematicians and she continues to inspire mathematicians worldwide. The American Mathematical Society has lectures named after her and in Iran the day of her death is now the National Day of Mathematics.

Her rich but short life testifies to her grit, grace and dedication to the pursuit of knowledge, an avocation that transcends political borders and gender lines. In her exceptional success Maryam Mirzakhani also embodied a sea change in the status of women in her native country. She created a life far larger than the official mandates of the Islamic Republic might typically allow. Her story exemplifies the idea that has shaped this book: women's history is human history.

# AFTERWORD

We have seen that in the history of Islam women have accomplished a lot more than domestic chores behind the veils of seclusion. One example after another has illustrated that women had historical agency, and has implied that such an agency deserves to be acknowledged in the past and encouraged for the future. Of course, the twenty-one women whose biographies shape this book were all extraordinary women. History often fails to document the lives of ordinary people – especially women. By comparison, we have far more abundant information about what presumably extraordinary men did. Even when a woman got to rule as queen and enjoy the highest status, her position hardly empowered her female subjects. However, ignoring or downplaying such cases in the past makes it harder to break new ground for female agency in the here and now.

No doubt, the record of women's participation in the history of Islam has been obscured by an overwhelming interest in the actions and achievements of caliphs, kings, and courtiers, coupled with a primary preference for the teachings of the *ulama*, Sufi masters, and other men of political and religious authority.

Organizing a narrative history of Islam in terms of women's lives poses challenges on multiple levels, both for methodology and content. Historically, the demands of politics, morality, and religion reinforced one another to give center stage to men and to sideline women. Especially in the past, Islamic societies did not encourage women to engage in the same activities as men in the same social class. The participation of women in public events was limited, and generally women scarcely enjoyed an equal status with men. Circumstances and outcomes seldom fit women's ideals or gave voice to them. However, at least before the nineteenth century, such discrepancy between women and men passed as normal almost everywhere in the world, not solely in Islamic societies.

The extant sources were almost entirely written by men, in whose works women were more likely to be "represented" than allowed to tell their own stories. Of course, male historians, chroniclers, and jurists have felt intrigued by women, especially famous women, and have produced extensive – but biased – information and numerous extant sources with a wealth of material about women's roles and legal status in the history of Islam.

Collections of biographical notices on women have a long pedigree in Islamic history, going back at least to the ninth-century work by Muhammad Ibn Sa'd (ca. 784–845) on the women of Madina. Ruth Roded's *Women in Islamic Biographical Collections* (1994) surveys this literary tradition.

Despite all this, the situation of women in most contemporary Muslim-majority countries today, from Afghanistan to Saudi Arabia and even in communities of Muslim migrants worldwide, remains far from ideal. Social restrictions, such as having females chaperoned by male relatives outside the house, as required in many Arab countries today, and policing women's dress in Iran, are all too familiar examples. Disparities in educational advancement, economic opportunity, and public engagement are no less alarming. It is often observed that Islamic or sharia law limits women's accepted roles. Legions of male writers of women's biographies, both from within Islamic societies and later the foreign Orientalists gazing from the outside, have shared unexamined, misogynistic, and self-contradictory assumptions about the nature of women. Their tainted premises are intellectually untenable and sometimes psychologically disturbing. For example, dismissing women's agency, they have depicted women as emotionally and physically fragile and intellectually feeble beings incapable of facing up to fierce reality.

Logical consistency is never a major concern for bigots. So the advocates of theories that routinely spoke of women as embodiments of passivity, coldness, and immobility, also espoused a diametrically opposite viewpoint when it suited them. Confronted by historical cases of a woman bursting upon the public scene and taking matters into her hands, they switched to an alternative theory that associated womanhood with wild, tempestuous, and impure and improper energies. Vacillating between such alternative but equally misinformed notions partly depended on the observer's own place in the power hierarchy. To sustain male dominance, such insiders and outsiders both identified women's empowerment as a sign and source of decline, bolstering the notion that women's rule brings destruction and fall. Of course, faced with exemplars of female piety, which the Islamic tradition broadly reveres, some had to acknowledge that male or female form does not matter in God's eyes and so it should not matter in men's eyes either. We saw examples of these positions throughout this book.

Today, society has changed, and so have the demands of politics and morality. So the proper place of women in the past, present, and future of Islam must be reconsidered in a new light. Such a reconsideration is both an intellectual necessity and a timely intervention in some of the urgent concerns of our time. Islam has a long and complex history and in this book I have tried to acknowledge and restore the distinct voice of women in it.

Excellent academic work has emerged on past and present. Since the 1980s the topic of women in Islam and in Islamic societies has been the focus of outstanding scholarship and has become part of the mainstream across disciplines such as history, anthropology, and political science. Hundreds of monographs and edited volumes have appeared on the subject. Our pool of primary sources and supplemental evidence has grown significantly, thanks in part to translations from Arabic, Persian, Turkish, Urdu, Malay, and Russian into English. Some primary sources have been re-examined in the light of women's history and feminist theory. The availability of reference works and specialized journals in English signals the ongoing relevance of this field of research worldwide. In the section on 'Further Reading' I cite a small sample of this literature, both to acknowledge my own intellectual debt and to introduce the interested reader to where more can be found, a lot more.

As stated in my Introduction, I have chosen to steer clear of polemics in general. However, one specific example deserves mention at this point. This book avoids the trodden path of limiting women's historical agency primarily to acts of resistance or defiance vis-à-vis male domination. This is important, but there are other books that emphasize women's acts of bravura, gambits, fearlessness, and secret lives in various Islamic communities and societies. A market exists for depictions of women both as delicate flowers or precious jewels and as relentless trailblazers or fierce warriors, but crediting women for resisting or rebelling against those who control their lives often depends on the assumption that those women possess some kind of feminist awareness and will-to-power, when such an awareness or intention may not always be present. Still, that is an important matter that deserves attention elsewhere.

As exemplified by many of the biographies in this book on individuals who lived prior to the twentieth century, women may both resist and support the existing tenets of power at the same time. Historical agency and social autonomy are often interrelated but may exist without each other as well; the reality of women's lives in the history of Islam remains just as complex and fascinating.

However, shedding more light on the place of women in the past, illuminating the present, and pointing the way toward a brighter future in which both men and women contribute to the betterment of the human condition in our world will require a lot more conscious, conscientious, and courageous effort than reading or writing a book.

# NOTES

## 1 Khadija

1 Alfred Guillaume, *Life of Muhammad* (1955, 1967), p. 106. See Quran sura 96, 'Alaq, verses 1–5. With this example as a guide, henceforth references to the Quran will appear in the following format, Q.Chapter name (chapter number): verse (s), e.g., Q.'Alaq (96): 1–5.

2 Ibid.

3 Guillaume, pp. 106–7.

4 Guillaume, pp. 82–3.

5 Q.Duha (93): 3–5.

6 Q.Duha (93): 6–8.

7 Q.Duha (93): 9–11.

8 Guillaume, p. 115.

9 Q.Takwir (81): 1–4.

10 Q.Takwir (81): 8–9.

11 Q.Takwir (81): 26–9.

12 Q.Humaza (104): 1–4.

## 2 Fatima

1 Fahmida Suleman, ed., *People of the Prophet's House: Artistic Ritual Expressions of Shi'i Islam: A Translation of Ibn Ishaq's Sirat Rasul-Allah* (2015), p. 183.

2 Wilferd Madelung, *The Succession to Muhammad: A Study of the Early Caliphate* (1997), p. 1.

3 Q.Nisa' (4): 7

4 Q.Isra' (17): 26.

5 Q.Kawsar (108). This is the shortest full chapter (*sura*) in the Quran.

## 3 Aisha

1  Q. Ahzab (33): 6.
2  Fatima Mernissi, *The Veil and the Male Elite: A Feminist Interpretation of Women's Rights in Islam* (1991), p. 78, text to footnotes 36, 37.
3  Aisha Geissinger, "Aisha bint Abi Bakr and Her Contributions to the Formation of the Islamic Tradition" (2011), p. 41; Mernissi, *The Veil and the Male Elite*, p. 77, text to footnote 34.
4  Q.Nur (24): 4.
5  Mernissi, pp. 69ff.
6  Ibid., p. 73 text to note 24.
7  Ibid., p. 78, text to note 38. My translation slightly differs from that in Mernissi.
8  Ibid., p. 70 text to footnote 11.
9  Geissinger, p. 41 text to note 39.
10  Mernissi, p. 49 text to footnote 1.
11  Ibid., p. 50 text to footnote 4.
12  Ibid., p. 53.

## 4 Rabia al-Adawiyya

1  See Richard Bulliet, *Cotton, Climate, and Camels in Early Islamic Iran: A Moment in World History* (2009).
2  For a different translation, see R. A. Nicholson, *A Literary History of the Arabs* (1930), p. 234.
3  Chase F. Robinson, *Islamic Civilization in Thirty Lives: The First 1,000 Years* (2016).
4  For a different translation, see Paul Losensky's rendition in Farid-al-Din Attar's *Memorial of God's Friends: Lives and Sayings of Sufis* (2009), p. 97.
5  Q.Yunus (10): 62–4.

## 5 Fatima of Nishapur

1  Asma Sayeed, *Women and the Transmission of Religious Knowledge in Islam* (2013).
2  Rkia Elaroui Cornell, introduction to Abu 'Abd al-Rahman as-Sulami, *Early Sufi Women: Dhikr an-niswa al-muta'abbidat as-Sufiyyat* (1999), pp. 54–60 and 142–5.
3  Richard Bulliet, "Women and the Urban Religious Elite in the Pre-Mongol Period" (2003), p. 68.
4  Qushayri, *Epistle on Sufism*, tr. Alexander D. Knysh (2007), p. 110.

## 7 Terken Khatun

1  Q.Nur (24): 4

# NOTES

## 8 Shajara'-al-Durr

1 David J. Duncan, "Scholarly Views of Shajarat al-Durr: A Need for Consensus" (2000), citing Sir John Glubb, *Soldiers of Fortune* (1973), pp. 49–50.
2 Amin Maalouf, *The Crusades Through Arab Eyes* (1986), p. 238.
3 Fatima Mernissi, *The Forgotten Queens of Islam* (1993), p. 90.

## 9 Sayyida al-Hurra of Tétouan

1 https://en.unesco.org/creative-cities/tetouan.
2 Mernissi, *Forgotten Queens*, p. 16.
3 Hasna Lebbady, *Feminist Traditions in Andalusi-Moroccan Oral Narratives* (2009).
4 Ibid.
5 Ibid.

## 10 Pari Khanum

1 Eskandar Beg Monshi-Turkaman, *History of Shah 'Abbas the Great* (1978), vol. I, p. 133.
2 Ibid., p. 292.
3 Ibid., p. 298.
4 Ibid., p. 298.
5 Rudi Mathee, *Pursuit of Pleasure: Drugs and Stimulants in Iranian History, 1500–1900* (2009), p. 104.
6 Monshi-Turkaman, p. 327. The translation given is mine.
7 Vladimir Minorsky, *Tadhkirat al-Muluk: A Manual of the Safavid Administration* (1943), p. 23.
8 Roger M. Savory, Ismail II, in *Encyclopaedia of Islam*.

## 11 Nur Jahan

1 Jahangir, *The Jahangirnama: Memoirs of Jahangir, Emperor of India* (1999), p. 40.
2 Cited in Ruby Lal, *Empress: The Astonishing Reign of Nur Jahan* (2018), p. 103.
3 M. K. Hussain, *Catalogue of Coins of the Mughal Emperors* (1968), p. 10.
4 Cited from Lal, *Empress*.
5 Cited in Lal, *Empress*, ch. 9, text to footnote 22.

## 12 Safiye Sultan

1 Leslie Penn Peirce, *The Imperial Harem: Women and Sovereignty in the Ottoman Empire* (1993), p. 95.
2 Maria Pia Pedani, "Safiye's Household and Venetian Diplomacy" (2000), p. 13.

3  Cited in Leslie Penn Peirce, *Empress of the East: How a European Slave Girl Became Queen of the Ottoman Empire* (2017), ch. 10, note 12; also, Peirce, *Imperial Harem*, p. 202.
4  Peirce, *Imperial Harem*, p. 223.
5  Clinton Bennett, "Correspondence with Safiye Sultan" (2015). See also Andrea Bernadette, *Women and Islam in Early Modern English Literature* (2007), p. 13.
6  Peirce, *Imperial Harem*, p. 228. Peirce, *Empress of the East*, text to note 41 in the final chapter before the epilogue.
7  Peirce, *Imperial Harem*, p. 126.
8  Bennett.
9  Peirce, *Imperial Harem*, pp. 242–3.
10  Ibid., p. 242.
11  Pedani, p. 15.
12  Peirce, *Imperial Harem*, p. 231.

# 13 Tajul-Alam Safiatuddin Syah

1  Marco Polo, *The Travels of Marco Polo* (1926), pp. 338, 341–2.
2  Q.Yunus (10): 25; An'am (6): 127.
3  Sher Banu A. L. Khan, *Sovereign Women in a Muslim Kingdom: The Sultanahs of Aceh, 1641–1699* (2017), pp. 66–92.
4  40 *bahar* (a Malay measurement of approximately 210–30 kg), so 2000 lb.
5  https://www.thirteen.org/dutchny/interactives/manhattan-island/.
6  On this hadith, see Chapter 3 on Aisha.

# 14 Tahereh

1  See note 66 in Moojan Momen, "Usuli, Akhbari, Shaykhi, Babi: The Tribulations of a Qazvin Family" (2003). Nabil Zarandi, *The Dawn-Breakers: Nabil's Narrative of the Early Days of the Baha'i Revelation* (1974), 63–66 (English translation 84n.). I have changed the translation.
2  Cf. Zarandi, p. 81, note 2, and p. 285, note 2. Certain lines, there translated by Shoghi Effendi, are incorporated here.
3  Momen, text to note 84.
4  Ibid., note 95 and text to note.1

# 15 Nana Asmau

1  Jean Boyd, "Distance Learning from Purdah in Nineteenth-Century Northern Nigeria: The Work of Asma'u Fodiyo" (2001). I have altered the translation.
2  Jean Boyd, "The Fulani Women Poets,", p. 128. Translation slightly modified here.

# NOTES

## 17 Halidé Edip

1 http://www.loc.gov/pictures/collection/ahii/.
2 Eric Zurcher, *Turkey: A Modern History* (2004), p. 128.
3 Edib Adivar, *Conflict of East and West in Turkey* (1963), p. 236.
4 Q.Nisa' (4): 32. Mushirul Hasan, *Between Modernity and Nationalism* (2010), pp. 60–1
5 Edib Adivar, p. 199.
6 Ibid., p. 201.
7 Edib Adivar, *Inside India* (1937).

## 18 Noor Inayat Khan

1 Shrabani Basu, *Spy Princess: The Life of Noor Inayat Khan* (2008), p. 39.
2 Ibid., p. 58.
3 Ibid., p. 60.
4 Ibid., p. 66.

## 19 Umm Kulthum

1 Virginia Danielson, *The Voice of Egypt: Umm Kulthum, Arabic Song, and Egyptian Society in the Twentieth Century* (1997, 2008), p. 243.
2 Ibid., p. 185.
3 Laura Lohman, *Umm Kulthum: Artistic Agency and the Shaping of an Arab Legend, 1967–2007* (2010).
4 https://www.youtube.com/watch?v=SgKTlAXgcTE.

## 20 Zaha Hadid

1 Zaha Hadid, "Being an Arab and a Woman Is a Double-edged Sword," interview by Huma Qureshi, *Guardian*, November 14, 2012, https://www.theguardian.com/lifeandstyle/2012/nov/14/zaha-hadid-woman-arab-double-edged-sword. Accessed May 17, 2018.
2 Ibid.
3 Ibid.
4 http://www.aub.edu.lb/aboutus/Pages/history.aspx.
5 "A Warped Perspective," *Daily Telegraph*, https://www.telegraph.co.uk/culture/art/ 3645888/A-warped-perspective.html.
6 Ibid.
7 "Foulath Hadid: Writer and Expert on Arab Affairs," *Independent*, October 12, 2012, https://www.independent.co.uk/news/obituaries/foulath-hadid-writer-and-expert-on-arab-affairs-8207992.html.
8 "2004 Pritzker Prize announcement," http://www.pritzkerprize.com/2004/announcement.
9 Deyan Sudjic, "Dame Zaha Hadid Obituary," *Guardian*, April 1, 2016, https://www.theguardian.com/artanddesign/2016/apr/01/zaha-hadid-obituary.

10 Interview by Huma Qureshi.
11 John Seabrook, "The Abstractionist," *The New Yorker*, December 21, 2009, https://www.newyorker.com/magazine/2009/12/21/the-abstractionist.
12 *Zaha Hadid*, (2016), p. 254.
13 Ibid., p. 1.

## 21 Maryam Mirzakhani

1 http://www.claymath.org/library/annual_report/ar2008/08Interview.pdf.
2 Section III, Principle XXX.
3 Roya Beheshti, "Maryam Mirzakhani in Iran." In *AMS Newsletter*, November 2018.
4 http://www.claymath.org/library/annual_report/ar2008/08Interview.pdf.
5 "Maryam Mirzakhani, Stanford Mathematician and Fields Medal Winner, Dies," *Stanford News*, https://news.stanford.edu/2017/07/15/maryam-mirzakhani-stanford-mathematician-and-fields-medal-winner-dies/. Accessed July 15, 2017.
6 "IMU Prizes 2014 citations," International Mathematical Union, 2014 citations.
7 http://www.claymath.org/library/annual_report/ar2008/08Interview.pdf.
8 Ibid.
9 Andrew Myers and Bjorn Carey, "Maryam Mirzakhani, Stanford Mathematician and Fields Medal Winner, Dies," *Stanford News*, 15 July 2017.
10 http://www.claymath.org/library/annual_report/ar2008/08Interview.pdf.
11 Graduate Students, *AMS Newsletter*, November 2018.
12 From ibid., pp. 1246–7.
13 Alex Eskin, in ibid.
14 Cumrun Vafa, in ibid.
15 http://www.claymath.org/library/annual_report/ar2008/08Interview.pdf.

# FURTHER READING

**Khadija (ca. 560–619 CE): The First Believer**
Accounts of Khadija's life are interwoven with the biographies of Prophet Muhammad. For an English translation of the earliest extant primary source, see *Life of Muhammad: A Translation of Ibn Ishaq's Sirat Rasul-Allah* by Alfred Guillaume (1967), especially pp. 82–3, 105–13, 191, 313. Images and descriptions in *The House of Khadeejah Bint Khuwaylid (may Allah be pleased with her) in Makkah al-Mukarramah: A Historical Study of its Location, Building, and Architecture*, which was published by the Furqan Islamic Heritage Foundation in London in 2014, cover some of the archeological excavations of the late 1980s in Mecca that unearthed the house of Khadija. For a brief and accessible biography, see also *Khadija: The First Muslim and the Wife of the Prophet Muhammad* by Resit Haylamaz. *Muhammad at Mecca* by William Montgomery Watt (1909–2006) contains references to other primary sources on the Prophet's days in Mecca.

## Fatima (ca. 612–633): The Prophet Muhammad's Flesh and Blood

Karen Ruffle explores the exemplary role of the father–daughter relationship of Fatima and the Prophet in her "May You Learn from Their Model: The Exemplary Father–Daughter Relationship of Mohammad and Fatima in South Asian Shiism" (2011). While she specifically focuses on Shias in South Asian history, most of the points she makes may in principle be extrapolated to other contexts. Laleh Bakhtiar's translation (1981) of the twentieth-century Shia writer Ali Shariati's influential book, *Fatima is Fatima*, provides a passionate insider's perspective. In *Fatima, Daughter of Muhammad* (2009), Christopher Clohessy presents a different view of biographical material on Fatima, from early Sunni and Shia sources in Arabic. He includes statements on the esoteric qualities in the annunciation of Fatima's birth, the motif of grief and suffering in her life, and more on her teachings and piety. The author considers parallels between some Shia depictions of the Prophet's daughter and Christian depictions of Mary, the mother of Jesus. This last topic is more deeply explored in *Chosen among Women* by Mary Thurlkill (2007). Firouzzeh Kashani-Sabet further examines historical representations of Fatima in her article "Who is Fatima? Gender, Culture, and Representation in Islam" (2005). On the issue of the succession, Fadak, and Fatima's protest, see Wilferd Madelung's *The Succession to Muhammad: A Study of the Early Caliphate* (1997) , especially, pp. 14–16, 21, 50–1, 62–4, and that book's index for more. William Montgomery Watt's *Muhammad at Medina* (1956) provides a detailed view of Prophet Muhammad's "ministry" in Medina derived from Arabic sources..

## Aisha (ca. 615–678): "Get Half of Your Religion from Her"

The biography of Aisha that Nadia Abbott (1897–1981) wrote decades ago, *Aishah, the Beloved of Mohammed* (1942), remains a good source. In her informative, well-researched, and theoretically aware monograph, *Politics, Gender, and the Islamic Past: The Legacy of*

*A'isha bint Abi* (1994), Denise Spellberg examines how Aisha's life and legacy have been variously interpreted by medieval Sunni and Shia Muslims. Aisha Geissinger summarizes existing research on Aisha's roles in the formation of some aspects of the early Islamic tradition in her "Aisha bint Abi Bakr and Her Contributions to the Formation of the Islamic Tradition." Again, W.M. Watt's *Muhammad at Medina* (1956) provides a detailed view of Prophet Muhammad's "ministry" in Medina. Fictional works have appeared on Aisha as well, including *Mother of the Believers*, in which Kamran Pasha takes the reader on an enjoyable ride.

## Rabia al-Adawiyya (ca. 717–801): The Embarrassment of Riches, and its Discontents

The most recent publication on Rabia of Basra, *Rabi'a from Narrative to Myth: The Many Faces of Islam's Most Famous Woman Saint, Rabi'a al-'Adawiyya* by Rkia Elaroui Cornell (2019) stands out as the most thorough study on this renowned female Sufi since Margaret Smith's (1884–1970) monograph (1994), *The Life and Work of Rabi'a and Other Women Mystics in Islam*. For primary source accounts of Rabia, see the biographical dictionary of women by Sulami, Abu 'Abd al-Rahman as-Sulami, *Early Sufi Women: Dhikr an-niswa al-muta'abbidat as-Sufiyyat* (1999), as well as Farid-al-Din Attar's *Memorial of God's Friends: Lives and Sayings of Sufis* (2009). The late Annemarie Schimmel (1922–2003), who was a leading authority on Sufism in the English-speaking world, wrote a classic on Sufism, *Mystical Dimensions of Islam*. Her *My Soul Is a Woman: The Feminine in Islam* (1997) contains more information on several female Sufis, notably on Rabia.

## Fatima of Nishapur (ca. 1000–1088): Keeper of the Faith

In his article, "Women and the Urban Religious Elite in the Pre-Mongol Period" (2003), Richard Bulliet provides an insightful analysis of Fatima, discussing the role she and other female hadith-transmitters played in large cities. For a study of women in hadith learning in general, see Asma Sayeed's *Women and the Transmission of Religious Knowledge in Islam* (2013). For a different perspective, see *Islamic Civilization in Thirty Lives: The First 1,000 Years* by Chase Robinson (2016), specifically the short biography there on a female hadith transmitter from a generation before Fatima. On women Sufis up to Fatima's generation, see Sulami's *Early Sufi Women* as well as Schimmel's *My Soul Is a Woman: The Feminine in Islam*. The treatise by Fatima's husband, Abu-l-Qasim al-Qushayri (ca. 1055), which is a classic on Sufi teachings, has been made available in an English translation by Alexander Knysh. For a detailed history of Nishapur during Fatima's lifetime and beyond, see Richard Bulliet's outstanding *Patricians of Nishapur: A Study in Medieval Islamic Social History* (1972).

### Arwa (ca. 1050–1138): The Queen of Sheba *Redux*

Delia Cortese and Simonetta Calderini provide plenty of information on Malika Arwa, particularly in chapter 4 of their monograph on *Women and the Fatimids in the World of Islam* (2006). For a discussion of contemporary reactions to Arwa's political and religious career, and how both Fatimid and local chroniclers felt uneasy about a woman occupying key political and religious positions, see Samer Traboulsi's translation of passages from some chronicles in "The Queen was Actually a Man: Arwa Bint Ahmad and the Politics of Religion" (2003). Marina Rustow presents a detailed study of a petition to a female member of the Fatimid court, analyzing it as an example of women's political authority under the Fatimid caliphate, in "A Petition to a Woman at the Fatimid Court" (2010).

### Terken Khatun (ca. 1205–1281): Doing Well and Doing Good

So far, the only scholarly treatment of Terken Khatun's life in the English language appears in Bruno de Nicolo's erudite monograph, *Women in Mongol Iran: The Kahtuns, 1206–1335* (2017).

## Shajara'-al-Durr (d. 1257): Perils of Power, Between Caliphs and Mamluks

In his "Scholarly Views of Shajarat al-Durr," David J. Duncan provides a good synopsis of perspectives on Shajara'-al-Durr, or Shajarat-al-Durr as some modern Arab authors prefer to write her name. Different views on this important woman are presented in Amalia Levanoni's article "Sagar Ad-Durr: A Case of Female Sultanate in Medieval Islam" (2001); Susan J. Staffa's "Dimensions of Women's Power in Historic Cairo" (1987); and Fatima Mernissi's book *The Forgotten Queens of Islam* (1993), pp. 90ff. Among the many popular history books by the prolific Lebanese writer Jurji Zaydan (1861–1914) that influenced the Muslim world view in modern times, one was a dramatized version of Shajara's life, *Zaydan*, which is made available in English as *Tree of Pearls, Queen of Egypt* (2012) thanks to the translator Samah Selim and Syracuse University Press. The popular book by the Lebanese writer Amin Maalouf, *The Crusades Through Arab Eyes* (1986), provides an engaging account of Shajara's time. For more on the general history of Mamluk rule in Egypt and Syria, see the collection of articles edited by Michael Winter and Amalia Levanoni, *The Mamluks in Egyptian and Syrian Politics and Society* (2004). R. Steven Humphreys' monograph, *From Saladin to the Mongols: The Ayyubids of Damascus 1193–1260* (1977), contains information directly relevant to Shajara's life, especially pp. 260–330.

## Sayyida al-Hurra of Tétouan (ca. 1492–ca. 1560): The Free Queen

In her *The Forgotten Queens*, Fatima Mernissi provided a pioneering modern account of the female ruler of Tétouan. For more recent literature, see the works of Hasna Lebbady on women in northern Morocco, including her scholarly monograph on *Feminist Traditions in Andalusi-Moroccan Oral Narratives* (2009), and her "Women in Northern Morocco: Between the Documentary and the Imaginary" (2012). Osire Glacier's *Political Women in Morocco:*

*Then and Now* (2013) also provides a broader understanding of the context.

## Pari Khanum (1548–1578): A Golden Link in the Safavid Chain of Command

Shohreh Golsorkhi's biographical account, "Pari Khan Khanum: A Masterful Safavid Princess" (1995) is a good place to look for more information, as are the two papers by Maria Szuppe, "The 'Jewels of Wonder': Learned Ladies and Princess Politicians in the Provinces of Early Safavid Iran" (1998), and "Status, Knowledge, and Politics: Women in Sixteenth-Century Safavid Iran" (2003). For a well-written recent fictional account of Pari Khanum's life, see Anita Amirrezvani's *Equal of Fire* (2012). In Michele Membrè's *Mission to the Lord Sophy of Persia (1539–1542)*, translated into English by A. H. Morton (1993), we have a Venetian merchant's eyewitness account of the Safavid state and court. For an English translation of a later Persian Safavid chronicle, see *History of Shah 'Abbas the Great* by Eskandar Beg Monshi-Turkaman. More on the historical background of the early Safavid era can be found in Rula J. Abisaab's *Converting Persia: Religion and Power in the Safavid Empire* (2015).

## Nur Jahan (1577–1645): Light of the World

On the reign of Nur Jahan, see the closely researched, vividly written, and accessible biography by Ruby Lal, *Empress: The Astonishing Reign of Nur Jahan* (2018).

## Safiye Sultan (ca. 1550–ca. 1619): A Mother of Many Kings

On the subject of women and political power in the Ottoman Empire, Leslie P. Peirce set a new standard with her monograph, *The Imperial Harem: Women and Sovereignty in the Ottoman Empire* (1993), and other works such as "Shifting Boundaries: Images of Ottoman Royal Women in the 16th and 17th

Centuries" (1988). Her more recently published *Empress of the East: How a European Slave Girl Became Queen of the Ottoman Empire* (2017) is more readily accessible for the general public. Maria Pia Pedani's study of "Safiye's Household and Venetian Diplomacy" (2000) and Nina Ergin's "Ottoman Royal Women's Spaces: The Acoustic Dimension" (2014) provide further valuable details.

### Tajul-Alam Safiatuddin Syah (1612–1675): Diamonds Are Not Forever

Sher Banu Khan's *Sovereign Women in a Muslim Kingdom: The Sultanahs of Aceh, 1641–1699* (2017) significantly enhances our understanding of the place of women in the history of Islam in early modern South-East Asia. This is the first full-length monograph to analyze female rule in Aceh, focusing in part on the first two decades of Tajul-Alam's rule, from 1636 to 1656.

### Tahereh (ca. 1814–1852): Heroine or Heretic?

Moojan Momen provides details on Tahereh's family background in "Usuli, Akhbari, Shaykhi, Babi: The Tribulations of a Qazvin Family" (2003). An account of Tahereh's life appears in Abbas Amanat's *Resurrection and Renewal: The Making of the Babi Movement in Iran, 1844–1850* (1989). For a rather different approach, see Negar Mottahedeh's "The Mutilated Body of the Modern Nation: Qurrat al-'Ayn Tahira's Unveiling and the Iranian Massacre of the Babis" (1998). Bahiyyih Nakhjavani reconstructs Tahereh's life in a work of literary fiction in *The Woman Who Read Too Much* (2015).

### Nana Asmau (1793–1864): Jihad and Sisterhood

In the English language we know about the works of Nana Asmau primarily thanks to the copious scholarship of Jean Boyd and Beverly B. Mack. The three monographs *Educating Muslim Women: The West African Legacy of Nana Asma'u 1793–1864* by Boyd and

Mack (2013), *One Woman's Jihad: Nana Asma'u, Scholar and Scribe* by Mack (2000), and Boyd's *The Caliph's Sister: Nana Asma'u, 1793–1865, Teacher, Poet, and Islamic Leader* (1989) provide a narrative background to Nana Asmau's life and times. The collection of writings translated into English (from Arabic, Fulfulde, and Hausa), *Collected Works of Nana Asma'u, Daughter of Usman dan Fodiyo (1793–1864)* (1997) provides primary source material enriched with notes and commentary by the editors Boyd and Mack.

### Mukhlisa Bubi (1869–1937): Educator and Jurist

We know more about Mukhlisa Bubi thanks to the recent scholarship of Rozaliya Garipova, in particular her recent articles "Muslim Female Religious Authority in Russia: How Mukhlisa Bubi Became the First Female *Qadi* in the Modern Muslim World" (2017); "Muslim Women's Religious Authority and Their Role in the Transmission of Islamic Knowledge in Late Imperial Russia" (2016); and "The Protectors of Religion and Community: Traditionalist Muslim Scholars of the Volga-Ural Region at the Beginning of the Twentieth Century" (2016). For background information, see Azade-Ayse Rorlich's *The Volga Tatars: A Profile in National Resilience* (1986); Shafiga Daulet's "The First All Muslim Congress of Russia: Moscow, 1–11 May 1917" (1989); Marianne Kamp's "Debating Sharia: The 1917 Muslim Women's Congress in Russia" (2015); and Agnés N. Kefeli's *Becoming Muslim in Imperial Russia: Conversion, Apostasy, and Literacy* (2014). On the Jadid Movement, see Edward J. Lazzerini's "Gadidism at the Turn of the Twentieth Century: A View from Within" (1975); Ingeborg Baldauf's "Jadidism in Central Asia within Reformism and Modernism in the Muslim World" (2001); Ahmet Kanlidere's *Reform within Islam: The Tajdid and Jadid Movement among the Kazan Tatars (1809–1917)* (1997); Adeeb Khalid's *Politics of Muslim Cultural Reform: Jadidism in Central Asia* (1999); and Dewin DeWeese's critical "It Was a Dark and Stagnant Night ('til the Jadids Brought the Light): Clichés, Biases, and False Dichotomies in the Intellectual

History of Central Asia" (2016). For further general background, see Robert Crews's *For Prophet and Tsar: Islam and Empire in Russia and Central Asia* (2009), especially pp. 31–91; Gregory J. Massell's *Surrogate Proletariat: Moslem Women and Revolutionary Strategies in Soviet Central Asia, 1919–1929* (1974); and Shoshana Keller's *To Moscow, Not Mecca: The Soviet Campaign against Islam in Central Asia* (2001).

## Halidé Edip (ca. 1884–1964): Author of the New Turkey

Halidé Edip (Adivar) paints a vivid self-portrait in her memoir, *The Turkish Ordeal* (1928). Erdag Göknar explores the complexities of her personality in "Turkish-Islamic Feminism Confronts National Patriarchy: Halide Edib's Divided Self" (2013). Arzu Öztürkmen offers a survey of women's activities during the transition from the Ottoman Empire to the Turkish Republic, in her "The Women's Movement under Ottoman and Republican Rule: A Historical Reappraisal" (2013). On women's education during the Late-Ottoman period, see Elizabeth B. Frierson's "Unimagined Communities: Women and Education in the Late-Ottoman Empire 1876–1909" (1995). For more background, see the volume edited by Duygu Köksal and Anastasia Falierou, *A Social History of Late Ottoman Women: New Perspectives* (2013). Serif Mardin's book, *The Genesis of Young Ottoman Thought; a Study in the Modernization of Turkish Political Ideas* (1962) is still informative, decades after it was written.

## Noor Inayat Khan (1914–1944): The Anxiety of Belonging

An engaging account of Noor Inayat Khan's story is set out in Shrabani Basu's *Spy Princess: The Life of Noor Inayat Khan* (2008).

## Umm Kulthum (ca. 1904–1975): Lodestar of Union

Two important works in English on Umm Kulthum are Virginia Danielson's *Voice of Egypt: Umm Kulthum, Arabic Song, and Egyptian*

*Society in the Twentieth Century* (2008) and Laura Lohman's *Umm Kulthum: Artistic Agency and the Shaping of an Arab Legend, 1967–2007* (2010).

## Zaha Hadid (1950–2016): Curves in Glass and Concrete

The little book entitled *Reflections on Zaha Hadid* contains a wealth of personal observations on Zaha Hadid and her artistic achievements. It can be seen at www.archdaily.com/785459/reflections-on-zaha-hadid-a-compilation-of-introductory-remarks.

## Maryam Mirzakhani (1977–2017): The Princess of Mathematics

Numerous obituaries and tributes were published in the days following Maryam Mirzakhani's death. A lively portrait emerges from the multiple entries in the November 2018 issue of the *American Mathematical Society (AMS) Newsletter*.

## Afterword

For discussion of the theoretical impulse that emphasizes women's gestures, attitudes, and actions that exhibit possible traits of "resistance," see Lila Abu-Lughod's "The Romance of Resistance: Tracing Transformations of Power through Bedouin Women" (1990) and *Veiled Sentiments: Honor and Poetry in a Bedouin Society* (2000), as well as her more recent scholarship. See also Saba Mahmoud's insightful *Politics of Piety: The Islamic Revival and the Feminist Subject* (2005).

# BIBLIOGRAPHY

Abbott, Nadia, *Aishah, the Beloved of Mohammed* (Chicago, IL: University of Chicago Press, 1942, reprinted 1985).

Abisaab, Rula Jurdi, *Converting Persia: Religion and Power in the Safavid Empire* (London and New York, NY: I.B. Tauris, 2015).

Abu-Lughod, Lila, "The Romance of Resistance: Tracing Transformations of Power through Bedouin Women," *American Ethnologist*, 17 (1), 1990, pp. 41–55.

———. *Veiled Sentiments: Honor and Poetry in a Bedouin Society* (Berkeley, CA: University of California Press, 2000).

Adivar, Halidé Edip, *The Turkish Ordeal: Being the Further Memoirs of Halidé Edib* (London: The Century Co., 1928).

———. *Inside India* (London: Unwin Brothers, 1937).

———. *Conflict of East and West in Turkey* (Lahore, S. M. Ashraf, 1935).

Amanat, Abbas, *Resurrection and Renewal: The Making of the Babi Movement in Iran, 1844–1850* (Ithaca, NY: Cornell University Press, 1989).

Amirrezvani, Anita, *Equal of Fire* (New York, NY: Scribner, 2012).

Anon., *Reflections on Zaha Hadid (1950–2016)* (London: Serpentine Gallery, 2016).

as-Sulami, Abu 'Abd al-Rahman, *Early Sufi Women: Dhikr an-niswa al-muta 'abbidat as-Sufiyyat*, ed. and tr. Rkia Elaroui Cornell (Louisville, KY: Fons Vitae, 1999).

Attar, Farid-al-Din, *Memorial of God's Friends: Lives and Sayings of Sufis*, tr. Paul Losensky (Mahwah, NJ: Paulist Press, 2009).

Baldauf, Ingeborg, "Jadidism in Central Asia within Reformism and Modernism in the Muslim World," *Die Welt des Islams*, 41 (1), 2001, pp. 72–88.

Basu, Shrabani, *Spy Princess: The Life of Noor Inayat Khan* (Stroud, UK: The History Press, 2008).

Beck, Lois and Nashat, Guity (eds), *Women in Iran from the Rise of Islam to 1800* (Urbana, IL: University of Illinois Press, 2003).

Beheshti, Roya, "Maryam Mirzakhani in Iran," *AMS Newsletter*, November 2018.

Bennett, Clinton, "Correspondence with Safiye Sultan," in D. Thomas (ed.), *Christian–Muslim Relations 1500–1900* (Brill, 2015), available online: http://dx.doi.org/10.1163/2451-9537_cmrii_COM_28511.

Bernadette, Andrea, *Women and Islam in Early Modern English Literature* (Cambridge, UK: Cambridge University Press, 2007).

Boyd, Jean, *The Caliph's Sister: Nana Asma'u, 1793–1865, Teacher, Poet, and Islamic Leader* (London and Totowa, NJ: F. Cass, 1989).

———. "Distance Learning from Purdah in Nineteenth-Century Northern Nigeria: The Work of Asma'u Fodiyo," *Journal of African Cultural Studies*, 14 (1), 2001, pp. 7–22.

Boyd, Jean and Mack, Beverly B., *Educating Muslim Women: The West African Legacy of Nana Asma'u 1793–1864* (Oxford and Leicester, UK: Interface Publications and Kube Publishing, 2013).

———. (eds), *Collected Works of Nana Asma'u, Daughter of Usman dan Fodiyo (1793–1864)* (East Lansing, MI: Michigan State University Press, 1997).

Bulliet, Richard W., *Patricians of Nishapur: A Study in Medieval Islamic Social History* (Cambridge, MA: Harvard University Press, 1972).

———. "Women and the Urban Religious Elite in the Pre-Mongol Period," in L. Beck and G. Nashat (eds), *Women in Iran from the Rise of Islam to 1800* (Urbana, IL: University of Illinois Press, 2003), pp. 68–79.

———. *Cotton, Climate, and Camels in Early Islamic Iran: A Moment in World History* (New York, NY: Columbia University Press, 2009).

Clohessy, Christopher Paul, *Fatima, Daughter of Muhammad* (Piscataway, NJ: Gorgias Press, 2009).

Cornell, Rkia Elaroui, *Rabi'a from Narrative to Myth: The Many Faces of Islam's Most Famous Woman Saint, Rabi'a al-'Adawiyya* (London: Oneworld Academic, 2019).

Cortese, Delia and Calderini, Simonetta, *Women and the Fatimids in the World of Islam* (Edinburgh: Edinburgh University Press, 2006).

Crews, Robert, *For Prophet and Tsar: Islam and Empire in Russia and Central Asia* (Cambridge, MA, and London: Harvard University Press, 2009).

Danielson, Virginia, *The Voice of Egypt: Umm Kulthum, Arabic Song, and Egyptian Society in the Twentieth Century* (Chicago, IL: University of Chicago Press, 1997, 2008).

# BIBLIOGRAPHY

Daulet, Shafiga, "The First All Muslim Congress of Russia: Moscow, 1–11 May 1917," *Central Asian Survey*, 8 (1), 1989, pp. 21–47.

de Nicolo, Bruno, *Women in Mongol Iran: The Kahtuns, 1206–1335* (Edinburgh: Edinburgh University Press, 2017).

DeWeese, Dewin, "It Was a Dark and Stagnant Night ('til the Jadids Brought the Light): Clichés, Biases, and False Dichotomies in the Intellectual History of Central Asia," *Journal of Economic and Social History of the Orient*, 59, 2016, pp. 37–92.

Duncan, David J., "Scholarly Views of Shajarat al-Durr: A Need for Consensus," *Arab Studies Quarterly*, 22, 2000, pp. 51–69.

Ergin, Nina, "Ottoman Royal Women's Spaces: The Acoustic Dimension," *Journal of Women's History*, 26 (1), 2014, pp. 89–111.

Frierson, Elizabeth B., "Unimagined Communities: Women and Education in the Late-Ottoman Empire 1876–1909," *Critical Matrix: Princeton Working Papers in Women's Studies*, 9 (2), 1995, p. 55.

Garipova, Rozaliya, "Muslim Women's Religious Authority and Their Role in the Transmission of Islamic Knowledge in Late Imperial Russia," *Tatarica*, 5, 2016, pp. 152–63.

———. "The Protectors of Religion and Community: Traditionalist Muslim Scholars of the Volga-Ural Region at the Beginning of the Twentieth Century," *Journal of Economic & Social History of the Orient*, 59, 2016, pp. 126–65.

———. "Muslim Female Religious Authority in Russia: How Mukhlisa Bubi Became the First Female *Qadi* in the Modern Muslim World," *Die Welt des Islams*, 57 (2), 2017, pp. 135–61.

Geissinger, Aisha, "Aisha bint Abi Bakr and her Contributions to the Formation of the Islamic Tradition," *Religion Compass*, 5 (1), 2011, pp. 37–49.

Gholsorkhi, Shohreh, "Pari Khan Khanum: A Masterful Safavid Princess," *Iranian Studies*, 28 (3–4), 1995, pp. 143–56.

Glacier, Osire, *Political Women in Morocco: Then and Now*, tr. Valérie Martin (Trenton, NJ: Red Sea Press, 2013).

Göknar, Erdag, "Turkish-Islamic Feminism Confronts National Patriarchy: Halide Edib's Divided Self," *Journal of Middle East Women's Studies*, 9 (2), 2013, pp. 32–57, 123.

Guillaume, Alfred, *Life of Muhammad: A Translation of Ibn Ishaq's Sirat Rasul-Allah* (Pakistan: Oxford University Press, 1955, 1967).

Hambly, Gavin R. G. (ed.), *Women in the Medieval Islamic World: Power, Patronage, and Piety* (New York, NY: St. Martin's Press, 1998).

Hasan, Mushirul, *Between Modernity and Nationalism: Halide Edip's Encounter with Gandhi's India* (New Delhi: Oxford University Press, 2010).

Haylamaz, Reşit, *Khadija: The First Muslim and the Wife of the Prophet Muhammad*, tr. Hülya Coşar (Somerset, NJ: Light, 2007).

Humphreys, R. Steven, *From Saladin to the Mongols: The Ayyubids of Damascus 1193–1260* (Albany, NY: State University of New York Press, 1977).

Husayn, Al-Hamdani, "The Life and Times of Queen Saiyidah Arwa the Sulaihid of the Yemen," *Journal of the Royal Central Asian Society*, 18, 1931, pp. 505–17.

Hussain, M. K., *Catalogue of Coins of the Mughal Emperors* (Bombay: Department of Archaeology, Government of Maharashtra, 1968).

Ibn Sa'd, Abu 'Abd-Allah Muhammad (ca. 784–845), *The Women of Madina*, tr. Aisha Bewley (London: Ta-Ha, 1995).

Jahangir, *The Jahangirnama: Memoirs of Jahangir, Emperor of India*, tr. Wheeler M. Thackston (Washington, D.C.: Freer Gallery of Art, Arthur M. Sackler Gallery: New York;, Oxford University Press, 1999).

Kamp, Marianne, "Debating Sharia: The 1917 Muslim Women's Congress in Russia," *Journal of Women's History*, 27 (4), 2015, pp. 13–37, 205–6.

Kanlidere, Ahmet, *Reform within Islam: The Tajdid and Jadid Movement among the Kazan Tatars (1809–1917)* (Istanbul: Eren, 1997).

Kashani-Sabet, Firoozeh, "Who Is Fatima? Gender, Culture, and Representation in Islam," *Journal of Middle East Women's Studies*, 1 (2), 2005, pp. 1–24.

Kefeli, Agnés Nilüfer, *Becoming Muslim in Imperial Russia: Conversion, Apostasy, and Literacy* (Ithaca, NY; London: Cornell University Press, 2014).

Keller, Shoshana, *To Moscow, Not Mecca: The Soviet Campaign against Islam in Central Asia* (Westport, CT: Praeger, 2001).

Khalid, Adeeb, *The Politics of Muslim Cultural Reform: Jadidism in Central Asia* (Berkeley, CA, Los Angeles, CA, and Oxford: University of California Press, 1999).

Khan, Sher Banu A. L., *Sovereign Women in a Muslim Kingdom: The Sultanahs of Aceh, 1641–1699* (Singapore: National University of Singapore Press, 2017).

Knysh, Alexander D., *Al-Qushayri's Epistle on Sufism: Al-Risala al-Qushayriyya fi 'ilm al-tasawwuf by Abu 'l-Qasim al-Qushayri*, tr. Alexander D. Knysh and reviewed by Muhammad Eissa (Reading, UK: Garnet Publishing, 2007).

Köksal, Duygu, and Falierou, Anastasia (eds), *A Social History of Late Ottoman Women: New Perspectives* (Boston, MA: Brill, 2013).

Lal, Ruby, *Empress: The Astonishing Reign of Nur Jahan* (New York, NY: W.W. Norton & Company, 2018).

Lazzerini, Edward J., "Gadidism at the Turn of the Twentieth Century: A View from Within," *Cahiers du Monde russe et soviétique*, 16 (2), 1975, pp. 245–77.

Lebbady, Hasna, *Feminist Traditions in Andalusi-Moroccan Oral Narratives* (New York, NY: Palgrave Macmillan, 2009).

# BIBLIOGRAPHY

————. "Women in Northern Morocco: Between the Documentary and the Imaginary," *Alif: Journal of Comparative Poetics*, 32, 2012, pp. 127–50.

Levanoni, Amalia, "Sagar Ad-Durr: A Case of Female Sultanate in Medieval Islam," in U. Vermeulan and D. De Smet (eds), *Egypt and Syria in the Fatimid, Ayyubid and Mamluk Eras*, vol. III (Leuven: Peeters Publishers, 2001), pp. 209–18.

Lohman, Laura, *Umm Kulthum: Artistic Agency and the Shaping of an Arab Legend, 1967–2007* (Middletown, CT: Wesleyan University Press, 2010).

Maalouf, Amin, *The Crusades Through Arab Eyes*, tr. Jon Rothschild [Fr. Orig., *Les Croisades vues par les Arabes* (1983)] (London: Al Saqi Books, 1986).

Mack, Beverly B., *One Woman's Jihad: Nana Asma'u, Scholar and Scribe* (Bloomington, IN: Indiana University Press, 2000).

Madelung, Wilferd, *The Succession to Muhammad: A Study of the Early Caliphate* (Cambridge, UK and New York, NY: Cambridge University Press, 1997).

Mahmoud, Saba, *Politics of Piety: The Islamic Revival and the Feminist Subject* (Princeton, NJ: Princeton University Press, 2005).

Mardin, Serif, *The Genesis of Young Ottoman Thought; a Study in the Modernization of Turkish Political Ideas* (Princeton, NJ: Princeton University Press, 1962).

Massell, Gregory J., *Surrogate Proletariat: Moslem Women and Revolutionary Strategies in Soviet Central Asia, 1919–1929* (Princeton, NJ: Princeton University Press, 1974).

Mathee, Rudi, *Pursuit of Pleasure: Drugs and Stimulants in Iranian History, 1500–1900* (Princeton, NJ: Princeton University Press, 2009).

Membrè, Michele, *Mission to the Lord Sophy of Persia (1539–1542)*, tr. A. H. Morton (London: University of London, 1993).

Mernissi, Fatima, *The Veil and the Male Elite: A Feminist Interpretation of Women's Rights in Islam*, tr. Mary Jo Lakeland (Reading, MA: Addison-Wesley Publishing Company, 1991).

————. *The Forgotten Queens of Islam* (Cambridge, UK, and Malden, MA: Polity Press, 1993).

Minorsky, Vladimir, *Tadhkirat al-Muluk: A Manual of the Safavid Administration* (London, 1943).

Momen, Moojan, "Usuli, Akhbari, Shaykhi, Babi: The Tribulations of a Qazvin Family," *Iranian Studies*, 36 (3), 2003, pp. 317–37.

Monshi-Turkaman, Eskandar Beg, *History of Shah 'Abbas the Great*, 2 vols, tr. Roger M. Savory (Boulder, CO: Westview Press, 1978).

Mottahedeh, Negar, "The Mutilated Body of the Modern Nation: Qurrat al-'Ayn Tahira's Unveiling and the Iranian Massacre of the Babis," *Comparative Studies of South Asia, Africa, and the Middle East*, 18, 1998, pp. 38–50.

Nakhjavani, Bahiyyih, *The Woman Who Read Too Much* (Stanford, CA: Redwood Press, 2015).

Nicholson, R. A., *A Literary History of the Arabs* (Cambridge, UK: Cambridge University Press, 1930).

Öztürkmen, Arzu, "The Women's Movement under Ottoman and Republican Rule: A Historical Reappraisal," *Journal of Women's History*, 25 (4), 2013, pp. 255–64.

Pasha, Kamran, *Mother of the Believers: A Novel of the Birth of Islam* (New York, NY: Washington Square Press, 2009).

Pedani, Maria Pia, "Safiye's Household and Venetian Diplomacy," *Turcica*, 32, 2000, pp. 9–32.

Peirce, Leslie Penn, "Shifting Boundaries: Images of Ottoman Royal Women in the 16th and 17th Centuries," *Critical Matrix: Princeton Working Papers in Women's Studies*, 4, 1988, pp. 43–82.

———. *The Imperial Harem: Women and Sovereignty in the Ottoman Empire* (New York, NY: Oxford University Press, 1993).

———. *Empress of the East: How a European Slave Girl Became Queen of the Ottoman Empire* (New York, NY: Basic Books, 2017).

Polo, Marco, *The Travels of Marco Polo*, tr. W. Marsden (London: J.M. Dent and Sons Limited, 1926).

Qushayri (ca. 1055). See Knysh 2007.

Reid, Anthony, "Female Roles in Pre-Colonial Southeast Asia," *Modern Asian Studies*, 22 (3), 1988, pp. 629–45.

Robinson, Chase F., *Islamic Civilization in Thirty Lives: The First 1,000 Years* (Berkeley, CA: University of California Press, 2016).

Roded, Ruth, *Women in Islamic Biographical Collections: From Ibn Saʻd to Who's Who* (Boulder, CO, and London: Lynne Rienner Publishers, Inc., 1994).

Rorlich, Azade-Ayse, *The Volga Tatars: A Profile in National Resilience* (Stanford: Hoover Institution Press, 1986)

Ruffle, Karen, "May You Learn from Their Model: The Exemplary Father–Daughter Relationship of Mohammad and Fatima in South Asian Shiism," *Journal of Persianate Studies*, 4 (1), 2011, pp. 12–29.

Rustow, Marina, "A Petition to a Woman at the Fatimid Court (413–414 A.H./1022–23 C.E.)," *Bulletin of the School of Oriental and African Studies*, 73 (1), 2010, pp. 1–27.

Sayeed, Asma, *Women and the Transmission of Religious Knowledge in Islam* (New York, NY: Cambridge University Press, 2013).

Schimmel, Annemarie, *Mystical Dimensions of Islam* (Chapel Hill, NC: University of North Carolina Press, 1975).

——— *My Soul is a Woman: The Feminine in Islam*, tr. Susan H. Ray (New York, NY: Continuum, 1997).

# BIBLIOGRAPHY

Shariati, Ali, *Ali Shariati's Fatima is Fatima*, tr. Laleh Bakhtiar (Tehran: Shariati Foundation, 1981).

Smith, Margaret, *The Life and Work of Rabi'a and Other Women Mystics in Islam* (Oxford: Oneworld Publications, 1994), revised form of a book originally published by Cambridge University Press, 1928.

Spellberg, Denise A., *Politics, Gender, and the Islamic Past: The Legacy of 'A'isha bint Abi Bakr* (New York, NY: Columbia University Press, 1994).

Staffa, Susan J. "Dimensions of Women's Power in Historic Cairo," in Robert Olson et al. (eds), *Islamic and Middle Eastern Societies: A Festschrift in Honor of Professor Wadie Jwaideh* (Brattleboro: Amana Books, 1987), pp. 62–99.

Suleman, Fahmida (ed.), *People of the Prophet's House: Artistic Ritual Expressions of Shi'i Islam* (London: Azimuth Editions in association with the Institute of Ismaili Studies, in collaboration with the British Museum's Department of the Middle East, 2015).

Szuppe, Maria "The 'Jewels of Wonder': Learned Ladies and Princess Politicians in the Provinces of Early Safavid Iran," in Gavin R. G. Hambly (ed.), *Women in the Medieval Islamic World* (Gordonsville, VA: Palgrave Macmillan, 1999), pp. 325–47.

———. "Status, Knowledge, and Politics: Women in Sixteenth-Century Safavid Iran," in L. Beck and G. Nashat (eds), *Women in Iran*, pp. 140–69.

Thurlkill, Mary F., *Chosen among Women: Mary and Fatima in Medieval Christianity and Shi'ite Islam* (Notre Dame, IN: University of Notre Dame Press, 2007).

Traboulsi, Samer, "The Queen was Actually a Man: Arwa Bint Ahmad and the Politics of Religion," *Arabica*, 50 (1), 2003, pp. 96–108.

Verde, Tom, "Sayyida al-Hurra," *Aramco World*, 2017, pp. 34–7.

Walther, Wiebke, *Women in Islam: From Medieval to Modern Times*, 3rd edn, tr. Guity Nashat (Princeton, NJ: Markus Wiener Publishing, 1993).

Watt, William Montgomery, *Muhammad at Mecca* (Oxford: Clarendon Press, 1953).

———. *Muhammad at Medina* (Oxford: Clarendon Press 1956).

Winter, Michael and Levanoni, Amalia (eds), *The Mamluks in Egyptian and Syrian Politics and Society* (Boston, MA: Brill, 2004).

Yamani, Ahmad Zaki, *The House of Khadeejah Bint Khuwaylid (may Allah be pleased with her) in Makkah al-Mukarramah: A Historical Study of its Location, Building, and Architecture* (London: Al-Furqan Islamic Heritage Foundation, 2014).

Zarandi, Nabil, *The Dawn Breakers: Nabil's Narrative of the Early Days of the Baha'i Revelation*, tr. Shoghi Effendi (Wilmette, IL: Baha'i Publishing Trust, 1974).

Zaydan, Jurji, *Tree of Pearls, Queen of Egypt*, tr. Samah Selim (Syracuse, NY: Syracuse University Press, 2012).

Zeynep, Basil Saydun, *Construction of Nationalism and Gender in Halidé Edib's Autobiographical Writings: Memoirs of Halidé Edib and The Turkish Ordeal* (Trier: WVT Wissenschaftlicher Veriag Trier, 2008).

Zurcher, Eric, *Turkey: A Modern History* (London: I.B. Tauris, 2004).

# ACKNOWLEDGMENTS

This book owes its existence to the generosity of many people who provided me with advice, criticism, and encouragement.

Thanks are due to Novin Doostdar and Juliet Mabey for publishing this book. At various points during the gestation of this work, Jonathan Bentley-Smith guided me with care and commitment, while Sam Carter's wise editorial recommendations raised the quality of my prose. Oneworld Publications proved to be the best publisher for me, and I am pleased to acknowledge the contributions of Anne Bihan, Hayley Warnham, Paul Nash, and other members of the team who helped shape this volume into what it is.

In all my thinking about history, I have learned immensely from Richard W. Bulliet and Ramzi Rouighi. I thank them both for decades of enriching camaraderie. With a combination of his unique insight and equally exceptional goodwill, Ramzi counseled me on the complexities of navigating diverse primary and secondary sources in multiple languages while keeping the historical narrative simple and straightforward. During our Thursday conversations over lunch, Richard urged me not to settle for

255

low-hanging fruit, and instead to dare to include biographies of lesser-known but still remarkable Muslim women from across the globe. They both read drafts of the manuscript and suggested significant improvements. Fayre Makeig also took her wonder-working pen to enhance the text of this book. I wish to thank Michael Berk and Rafia Ahmad for each reading an earlier draft of one of the chapters.

I am grateful to Brinkley Messick and Astrid Benedek for granting me affiliation with the Middle East Institute at Columbia University and facilitating my access to library resources, which were indispensable for my research. I pay tribute to the priceless devotion of librarians everywhere, including those at Columbia University, as well as local librarians in Larchmont and New York City.

I consider it a blessing to savor the abundant benevolence of my community of friends in Westchester County, NY, and Fairfield County, CT. Specifically, I wish to express my sincere appreciation to Ms. Shireen Mahallati, Dr. Hossein Sadeghi, Dr. Golnar Raisi-Sadeghi, and others for welcoming me into their homes. Among this group, Mrs. Maria Dolores Paoli unstintingly shared dozens of books on women in Islam from her personal library to help me with the writing of this work.

Here, I cherish the memory of my late aunt, Behjat Ashrafi, who passed away shortly after I had started writing this book. As noted on the dedication page, I owe her an unrepayable debt for her unconditional love and grace. Finally, I thank my family. Mitra, Mojdeh, Mohammad, and Reza give me the courage, consolation, and hope that I need to live.

# INDEX

257

# INDEX